THE SENSUOUS VEGETARIAN BARBECUE

VICKI RAE CHELF
DOMINIQUE BISCOTTI

Avery Publishing Group

Garden City Park, New York

Cover Design by Bill Gonzalez and Rudy Shur
Cover Photo by Mike Silva
Illustrated by Vicki Rae Chelf
In-house editor: Linda Comac
Paste-up: Marie Caratozzolo
Typesetter: Bonnie Freid

Library of Congress Cataloging-in-Publication Data

Chelf, Vicki Rae
    The sensuous vegetarian barbecue / by Vicki Rae Chelf and
Dominique Biscotti.
        p. cm.
    Includes index.
    ISBN 0-89529-613-6
    1. Vegetarian cookery. 2. Barbecue cookery. I. Biscotti,
Dominique. II. Title.
TX837.C4527 1994   94-13375
                                                         CIP

Copyright © 1994 by Vicki Rae Chelf and Dominique Biscotti

Printed in the United States of America

10 9 8 7 6 5 4 3 2

Contents

Foreword

Many people love to barbecue. Across America, from late May until September, you'll find families grilling outdoors. Most commonly, they are barbecuing chicken.

But check hospital records for food poisonings and you'll find something remarkable: The rate of food poisonings begins to rise in late May and June and stays high until September, when it drops back down to winter levels.

The reason, evidently, is that Americans are under-cooking the chicken on their grills. Barbecuing tends to scorch the outside of the meat quickly, but the insides remain under-cooked and contaminated with salmonella, campolybacter, and other pollutants.

And there are more problems with grilling chicken and other meats: Barbecuing produces carcinogenic compounds. Polynuclear aromatic hydrocarbons (PAHs) are formed when burning fat drips into an open flame. Heterocyclic aromatic amines (HAAs) are formed when amino acids and creatinine (a chemical found in muscles) react at high temperatures.

How dangerous are these substances? "If HAAs were regulated by federal agencies, they would have been banned yesterday," says Richard Adamson, director of the National

Cancer Institute's division of cancer etiology. Vicki Chelf and Dominique Biscotti's *The Sensuous Vegetarian Barbecue*, therefore, is an important book.

There are today so many reasons why people are moving in a more vegetarian direction. Some are doing so for their health; others, out of concern for the animals; others, because they want to help protect the environment, and still others from their concern for the world's hungry. But whatever your reasons, there always remains the question: What, then, do you eat?

As this book demonstrates, when you get that hunk of animal flesh off your plate, it leaves a lot of room for other wonderful foods.

Enjoy your food, and enjoy your life. And know that when you "go veggie," your body will thank you for the rest of your life.

—John Robbins
author of *Diet for a New America*
and founder of Earthsave Foundation

Introduction

What did the gods and goddesses of world mythology have in common with us? They loved to eat, drink, and make merry. Their food and drink—nectar and ambrosia—conjure up images of truly sensual delights. Eating is, of course, a sensual experience. We didn't need the eating scene in Fielding's bawdy novel *Tom Jones* to convince us that each sense plays a role in the eating experience. Anyone who has ever had a bad cold knows that without the sense of smell, we really don't taste our food. The importance of our sense of sight is now being recognized and emphasized by nouveau cuisine chefs. And isn't the crunch of food one of the most satisfying sounds you know?

With this in mind, one realizes that vegetarian dining may well be the only sensual pleasure that is completely free from vice. And it may be an even more sensual experience than other forms of eating. Fruits and vegetables offer an absolute riot of colors, aromas, and tastes. In addition, vegetarian dining helps to ensure good health, and we can only fully appreciate life's pleasures when we are healthy. Preparing the recipes in this book will help you to become truly sensual. After all, barbecuing involves flames—the universal symbol of passion. Now, add "a jug of wine, a loaf of bread," and your love beside you—you'll have Omar Khayyam's Paradise for sure.

Join us in a culinary adventure that will virbrate your senses. Discover all the healthy foods that can be cooked on an outdoor grill while you create a new tradition.

In the past, backyard cookouts created lots of precious memories: summer vacations, pool parties, Fourth of July, and times spent with friends and family enjoying our favorite foods. In the past few years, however, these pleasant traditions have lost some of their appeal. As we learn more and more about the importance of a low-fat and low-cholesterol diet for good health, we realize that many of the favorite foods of our past are perfect examples of the worst possible foods to eat. Discover vegetarian barbecuing and you needn't feel either guilty or deprived.

ENTER THE SENSUOUS WORLD
OF VEGETARIAN BARBECUING

Vegetables cooked on the grill have a different flavor and texture than vegetables cooked by steaming or boiling. Not only do they have that special smoky flavor that grilling provides, but searing seems to lock vegetables' natural flavors inside. Sweet vegetables taste sweeter when they are grilled. Just add a simple marinade or basting sauce and you will have a real taste treat. No wonder grilled vegetables are the rage today! You can't go into any good restaurant without finding grilled vegetables on the menu.

But vegetables are not the only foods that we use in vegetarian barbecue cooking. Tofu, tempeh, and seitan (traditional foods from the Orient) are perfect for grilling. They can be grilled with various marinades, served in numerous forms, and accompanied by a variety of scrumptious low-fat and no-cholesterol sauces and condiments. As we were experimenting with the recipes for this book, we were surprised over and over again at the versatility of grilling and the opportunity that it offers for creative cooking.

Soups and stews made from grilled foods have a richness of flavor that is extraordinary. They are great for entertaining because they can be made early in the day and heated up just before serving. Whole-wheat pizza and focaccia made on the grill have crispy bottom crusts and soft, tender middles that are not possible in the oven. They cook in less than ten minutes, too.

Salads made of grilled vegetables will add a gourmet touch to your meal. Take a grilled salad to a pot luck meal and wait for the compliments. Grilled sandwiches or pâtés made from grilled foods will probably make you forget that you ever enjoyed hamburgers, but if they don't, try grilling Yves Veggie Cuisine Burgers or hot dogs. Add some homemade relish and mustard, and you could fool almost anyone.

We even have recipes for desserts. A light and fluffy whole-wheat cake served with a sweet sauce and grilled fruits makes a truly luscious end to a perfect summer meal. Or try our natural sorbets and light pies that go wonderfully with grilled foods—or anything else.

You can easily find—and just as easily follow—the recipes for all these foods. Chapter headings include Appetizers, Salads, Main Dishes, Desserts, etc. When writing the recipes, we did not assume that you already know how to cook. Everything is explained so that even the novice can follow a recipe without difficulty.

If you are already accustomed to cooking with natural foods, you will find our ingredients familiar. If you are an experienced grill cook but are new to natural foods, you may find that recipes include ingredients with which you are unfamiliar; just look them up in Stocking Your Shelves (pages 19–28). This section will tell you everything you need to know about those foods. If you do not know much about grilling techniques, please read Grilling Basics (pages 13–17) and watch for the grilling tips scattered throughout the book. There are things you should know that cannot be said in every recipe.

If you have never bought a grill, you may want to read pages 5–11. There is also a section on the utensils and accessories needed for grilling, as well as information on cleaning and storing a grill.

Vegetarian grilling is fun, easy, and delicious, so please

join us and experience the inviting aroma, delightful flavors, and good times of healthy outdoor cooking. Let your future memories be of healthy foods, and help to create new traditions for tomorrow.

Equipment Facts

The grills on which we tested our recipes are simple, inexpensive gas grills. We chose gas because it is quicker and easier to use, and because most people have gas grills. Charcoal grills cook with lower heat. This can be an advantage, because foods are less likely to burn, but it can also be a disadvantage because it takes thirty to forty-five minutes just for the fire to reach the proper temperature for cooking. It also takes a bit of skill to get the fire started. Charcoal fans all agree, however, that the taste of charcoal grilling is superior, and they think that it is worth the extra time. All of our recipes can be cooked on either charcoal, gas, or electric grills.

BUYING A GRILL

There are as many kinds of grills as there are prices. The price of gas grills ranges anywhere from $100 to $5,000. Charcoal grills can be obtained for far less money, but brick barbecues can be quite expensive. The differences among these grills are the materials from which they are constructed, the way they are assembled, and their sizes. A more expensive grill will usually be made from thicker, better quality steel, and it will probably be better assembled. An inexpensive grill will not

last very long in the South, but will last a few years longer in
the North or Mid-West. After two years, my grill in Florida
needed a new burner (which can be purchased at hardware
stores), but Dominique's grill in Quebec is still good after three
years. A $100 grill will more than likely have to be assembled
by the buyer, and if the buyer is not extremely mechanically
adept, it's not worth the savings. Dominique and I both tried
to assemble our own and ended up getting help. In general, it
is okay to spend more if you are an experienced barbecuer
looking for performance and durability.

When deciding on a grill, you should be aware of the
various types on the market:

Portables or table-top models

These grills are 12–18 inches in diameter and include minature
covered gas, electric, and charcoal barbecues. A hibachi, the
Japanese word for fire bowl, is also in this category and is ideal
for beginners because it is safe and inexpensive. Cast-iron
hibachis are the best quality; pressed steel is not as durable.
Hibachis are available in single, double, or triple sizes and
should have vents in the fire bowl. A similar grill is the
Mexican brasero, which is really a ceramic hibachi.

A portable gas grill is fine for camping, and many of our
recipes can be made on one (except, perhaps, the pizza recipes,
which would not fit onto a portable or table-top grill) but for
home use and for entertaining, it is not appropriate. It does not
have a top rack and is too small to accommodate an entire recipe
at one time.

Braziers

A charcoal grill that is really a fire box and grill rack on a stand,
a brazier can be any uncovered charcoal grill on legs (the less
expensive ones often have shaky legs, which can be dangerous). These grills may be rectangular or kettle-shaped with
rounded undersides; it is harder to clean ashes from the rectangular type. For successful barbecuing, braziers should have
a charcoal rack, which allows air flow around the fire and lets

ash drop away from burning charcoal. Hooded braziers have half the grilled surface enclosed. This allows foods to be correctly cooked without the cook's constant attention. The hood is also a windshield. Place it towards the wind so smoke will not get in your eyes. Half-hooded braziers are equipped with rotisseries, either electric or battery-powered.

Wagon barbecue

Essentially a brazier, a wagon barbecue is rectangular in shape and mounted on a wheeled trolley that has work surfaces and shelves.

Brick barbecue

Usually custom-made, brick barbecues never corrode and look lovely on patios built of brick or stone. Be certain that your brick barbecue has sufficient airflow and that the correct size grill and racks are available. Pave the area under and immediately around the barbecue to protect it and provide a safe surface on which to work.

Covered charcoal grills

These covered barbecues have rounded bottoms for even heat distribution and are available in square, rectangular, or kettle shapes. The cover creates an ovenlike environment for roasting, smoking, or steaming. Covered charcoal grills should have adjustable racks and must have air vents in the base and lid. Many can be fitted with rotisserie attachments. The smaller units do not hold enough fuel to maintain stable heat.

Covered gas grills

More expensive than other types of grills, covered gas grills have the unfailing ability to maintain even, medium heat through long periods of cooking. There is usually a fire grate near the burners that holds lava rocks, pumice stones, or ceramic bricks. Newer designs have what is called "flavor bars." As far as cooking goes, all of these give the same results.

Their function is to catch the juices when they drop from the food. When the juice falls onto the rocks, stones, or flavor bars, it creates smoke that flavors the food.

Electric grills

Because they create no fumes, electric barbecues are suitable for indoor or outdoor use and come in table-top models for the kitchen and larger ones for the patio. To use this type of barbecue, you must have access to an electric power source.

Electric grills normally do not have covers. They consist of a metal box with an electric heating element about one-half inch from the bottom of the box. A bed of volcanic rocks touches the element.

Once you have decided on the type of grill you want, it's time to get down to details:

- Your grill should have two cooking racks. The bottom rack is used for quick-cooking foods, and the top rack is used for foods that require longer cooking or burn easily. This top rack is essential for cooking pizza, cakes, and slow-cooking vegetables, which will burn on the bottom rack, even with the heat turned down as low as it will go.

- If the grill has only one rack, you should be able to raise and lower the height to regulate the cooking temperature. This should be easy to do when the rack is full. The mechanism that raises and lowers the cooking rack should be placed so that it doesn't get too hot to handle.

- Gas grills should have a gauge that indicates hot, medium, and low temperature. This lets you know when the grill is ready and whether it is getting too hot.

- A shelf attached to the side of the grill is very handy. This is something that we use every time we grill. It will hold oil, basting liquid, trays, spatula, etc.

- Two burners help in controlling the heat. If something is cooking too quickly, one burner can be turned off and the food moved over to that side.

- No matter what kind of grill you choose, remember that for safe and comfortable barbecuing, you shouldn't have to bend too much or reach too far.
- The ideal grill will not have too many nuts and bolts that might fall out and cause a potential hazard.
- Chrome or nickle-plated steel are the ideal components for your grill. Porcelain or enamelled steel may chip if handled roughly. Cast aluminum or cast-iron are heavier but more durable and are often quite expensive.

CARE AND CLEANING OF YOUR GRILL

After grilling, it is always a good idea to clean the cooking grid or rack of the grill while it is still slightly warm. A heavy-duty scrubbing pad that is sold for scrubbing pots and pans is sufficient for this. Let the grill cool down until it is no longer burning hot but is still warm. Scrub the rack, right on the grill, to remove most of the residue. Then place it in a sink and scrub it with a little dish detergent and water. Rinse it in clear water.

If foods stick and burn while you are cooking on a gas grill and the rack needs to be quickly cleaned, just turn the grill off. Crumple up a sheet of aluminum foil and use this to scrub the rack while it is still on the grill. Be sure to wear an oven-mitt.

When charcoal grilling, you can simply let your barbecue burn out. To save the briquettes for later use, scatter sand or gravel to put out the fire. Lift unburned charcoal with long-handled metal tongs, and store in a metal bucket. Always empty the ash after using the grill. The sanitation department recommends putting ashes in a plastic bag and closing it securely. Loose ashes will stay in the hopper of the garbage truck and present a health hazard to workers on the truck who continually breathe the ashes.

If you cook on an electric grill, clean the rocks by heating them to high and leaving them for ten minutes after cooking.

You needn't worry about bacteria building up in a grill. Each time you preheat the grill, the temperature is so high that it kills any bacteria that may have formed between uses.

Before storing a grill for winter, take both the cooking grid and the fire grid off and clean the inside of the grill thoroughly. Brush the fire grid with a wire brush. The lava rocks or pumice stones may be cleaned by swishing them around in a sink full of soapy water.

If the grill is to be stored outside, place it under an over-hang or in a carport if possible, and cover it with a plastic cover. If a gas grill is to be stored indoors, remove the propane tank. Store the tank outside, or in a shed, away from the house.

ACCESSORIES NEEDED FOR GRILLING

It is not necessary to buy lots of accessories and gadgets for good grill cooking, but a few really are useful and some are absolutely necessary:

- A special rack with small holes for grilling small foods, some-times called a "Griffo Grill." Small foods, such as vegetables and sliced fruits, will fall through the spaces in the cooking grid of the grill. Therefore, for vegetable grilling, it is abso-lutely essential to have the rack with small holes. In recipes where this rack is needed, the text will read, "Place a rack with small holes on the bottom rack of the grill."

  These racks may be purchased at any store that sells grills and grilling accessories, or from mail-order catalogues that specialize in grilling.

- Long insulated oven-mitts. Grilling will be much more pleasant with the proper oven-mitts. The heat gets so high that it is sometimes difficult to turn foods over or remove them from the grill with regular pot holders.

- Long-handled spatula and forks for turning your grilled delicacies. Long-handled tongs also come in handy.

- Aluminum foil. Heavy-duty foil is used to make little pack-ets for grilling vegetables (especially vegetables that take longer to cook, such as potatoes, beets, artichokes, etc.). It is also used as a cover for such foods as pizza, cake, and stuffed vegetables.

- Bamboo skewers for kebobs. These seem to work better for

vegetarian cooking than the metal ones because they are smaller and do not break the food.

- A small brush for basting and oiling foods. It is essential to have a small brush, and it is nice to also have a larger brush to lightly oil the cooking racks.

- A metal ovenproof pan. We use an enamel cake pan. Do not try to use Pyrex or ceramic on the grill. The high temperature may break it.

- A plastic cover to protect the grill. This cover is essential unless you plan to store your grill indoors. If the grill is to be stored indoors, first remove the propane bottle. It should be kept outside or in a shed that is separate from the house.

- Charcoal. Many backyard chefs use charcoal briquettes, which are made by crushing hardwood charcoal and re-forming it with something—often cornstarch—to bind it. Because the old-fashioned kind is twice as dense as the modern quick-burning variety, it takes longer to start a fire and longer to reach correct cooking temperature.

  Pure hardwood coals or "lump charcoal" is expensive and hard to find. Pieces of lump charcoal burn hot and fast so they are best used in heavy-duty equipment. With constant use, they may burn right through your fire bowl. These coals also produce flying sparks. If you cook an entire meal rather than one course using lump charcoal, you will need to remake the fire before you are finished cooking.

- Fire starters. You can purchase either liquid, jellied, or electrical fire lighters for use with charcoal fires. Electrical fire lighters are more convenient to use than liquid or jellied fire lighters and are less expensive in the long run. Buy one once, and it will last for years. It may, however, be difficult to have a source of electricity near the barbecue.

Grilling Basics

The most basic aspect of grilling is starting the fire. The steps involved are different for charcoal, gas, and electric grilling.

STARTING CHARCOAL BARBECUES

1. Line the fire bowl with heavy duty foil. (This will prolong grill life and make it easier to remove ashes.)

2. Position a pyramid of charcoal in the center.

3. Ignite.

Using a liquid fire lighter: Carefully pour or spray the fluid onto a pyramid of charcoal. Do not let any collect in the bottom of the fire bowl. Allow the liquid to permeate the charcoal before igniting with a long match or taper.

Using a jellied fire lighter: You needn't worry about jelly accumulating in the base of the fire bowl. Put several teaspoons of jelly between the charcoals in the base of the pyramid. Wait a minute or so and ignite as above.

Using an electric fire lighter: Place the loop of the heating element near the base of the charcoal pyramid.

Turn the unit on or plug it in and wait five to ten minutes until the fire is going.

4. When a dusting of gray ash appears on the surface of the charcoal, the fire is ready. Spread charcoal out to cover the grill. (If you are using lump charcoal, you will need to wait fifteen to twenty minutes before you can cook. With briquettes, you will have to wait thirty to forty minutes.)

5. If the fire needs to be remade during cooking, place new charcoal around the outside of the fire. Move it toward the center when it is lit.

6. If the temperature needs to be increased, open all the vents, push coals into the middle, and tap off the ashes.

STARTING GAS BARBECUES

1. Be sure the gas bottle is properly connected.

2. Open the gas bottle.

3. Light a long match and insert into the air slot or the place recommended by the manufacturer.

4. Turn the gas control nob to high. If gas does not ignite immediately, turn off control nob and remove cover. *Do not* attempt to relight before three to five minutes have passed.

5. Preheat the grill, but not too much. (Most gas grills take from six to eight minutes to get hot. A gas grill will get much hotter than it needs to be if left on high.) Put the cover on and leave the temperature on high for about eight minutes. Most gas grills have a heat indicator with a needle that points to low, medium, and high; let the needle go to medium, or just under, then turn the gas as low as it will go. This should be perfect for most foods.

STARTING ELECTRIC BARBECUES

1. Plug in or turn on the barbecue.

2. Wait ten minutes before cooking so the rocks can heat.

BRING ON THE FOOD

Almost all vegetables can be cooked on the grill. Quick-cooking and thinly sliced vegetables can be grilled directly on the cooking grid of the grill or on a specially designed rack with small holes that can be placed on the cooking grid. Slower-cooking vegetables, such as root vegetables, can be wrapped in foil and cooked on the top rack of the grill.

The most important thing to remember about cooking vegetables on the grill is to watch them carefully. Onions, bell peppers, and other sliced or chopped vegetables need frequent stirring and turning to assure even cooking and to keep them from burning. Slower-cooking vegetables and vegetables in foil need to be moved around on the rack and turned from time to time for the same reason.

If you are new to grilling, you must remember that you are learning a new skill. Don't get discouraged if foods do not come out perfectly the first time. This is not to say that you can't make a great grilled meal on the first try. You can. Most of these recipes are so easy that you can't go wrong, but some are a little more difficult. It took us about four tries to make a perfect pizza. We didn't realize that it would be done on the grill in about eight minutes. Until we got our timing right, we burnt a few. Now that we know that it cooks so fast, we make perfect pizza every time.

You have an advantage because we give approximate times for all of our recipes, times we had to learn through trial and error. Still, no two grills are exactly the same so there is a little bit of intuition involved, which will improve with experience.

Listed below are some tips that we hope will help you to make great grilled meals right from the start:

- Watch the food carefully. The most common mistake among novices is burning of food. Even though we give approximate times, it is impossible to be exact. Grilling time can vary with the type of grill used. These recipes were tested on a gas grill; with a charcoal grill, each recipe will require longer cooking. The size of the food, and the temperature of the grill also make a difference. Therefore, the times are indicated to give you an idea, but it is just as important to use your own judgment. Sometimes, all it takes is a minute for a dish to go from beautiful golden brown to burnt.

- To test for doneness in vegetables, insert a bamboo skewer or fork into the vegetable. If it enters easily, the vegetable is done.

- Always soak bamboo skewers in water for one hour before using them for kebobs. This will keep the bamboo from burning.

- Grills may have "hot spots," or places where food cooks and burns faster than other places. You can avoid hot spots somewhat by making sure that the lava rocks in the bottom of a gas grill are evenly distributed. Bare places with no rocks are much hotter. But even with the rocks well distributed, the foods in the center of the grill tend to cook faster.

- If you see that food browns faster in a certain spot on the grill, move the food around as it cooks. This will help to keep it from burning. If foods are burning on the bottom rack, they can also be moved to the top rack.

- Sometimes, a gas grill gets too hot, and no matter where you place the food, it cooks too fast. If this happens, just turn off one or both of the burners. If you turn off one of the burners, move the food over to that side of the grill. If the grill cools down too much, just relight the burner.

- Unless you are turning or stirring food, keep the top of the grill closed. This assures more even cooking.

- Vegetables, particularly chopped onions and chopped bell peppers, need almost constant stirring to keep them from burning. Closing the top of the grill will help them to cook, but don't close it for too long or they might burn.

- Most gas grills have both a top and bottom rack. Use the bottom rack for foods that cook fairly quickly, and use the top rack for foods that require long, slow cooking, such as potatoes, sweet potatoes, beets, stuffed vegetables, etc. Also use the top rack for foods that burn easily, such as pizza and cakes.

    If your grill does not have two racks, it may have different placement levels for one rack. When the bottom rack is called for, place the rack near the flames or coals, and when a recipe calls for the top rack, move it up to the top level.

- Keep your grill racks clean. The black buildup that forms on the rack does not add flavor to the foods, it just makes them stick and burn. (See pages 9–10 for cleaning instructions.)
- Have everything prepared before you start grilling. Make sure that vegetables are chopped, kebobs are made, sauces and relishes are ready, etc. Have any foods that do not need grilling ready to serve because when you start grilling, it will require your full attention.
- When you have finished cooking, turn off the gas and allow the barbecue to completely cool. Shut down the gas valve. Remove the gas bottle and store it in a well ventialated area.

SAFETY TIPS

- If using a kettle grill, leave the cover on while grilling.
- Be sure the legs of your grill are level and steady so that the barbecue will not fall over if tipped slightly.
- Grill well away from trees, houses, sheds, and other flammable items.
- Keep small children and pets away from the grill.
- *Never* add lighter fluid to burning coal or a lighted fire. The fire will burn along the stream of the fluid, back to the can. You can be seriously injured.
- The legs of the barbecue should not extend too far beyond the cooking or grill area.
- The grill should not be constructed with too many nuts and bolts that might fall out thereby creating a hazard.
- Use only lighter fluids manufactured for barbecue use. *Never* use petroleum, lighter fuel, naphta, paraffin, or kerosene.

Stocking Your Shelves

The dishes in this book are prepared using all-natural vegetarian ingredients. Since milk and dairy products are derived from animals, they are not used in our recipes. In some cases, we do use commercially prepared substitutes. "Stocking Your Shelves" lists the less common ingredients that you will need; they can be purchased in most natural foods stores. If you are not familiar with an ingredient that is used in one of our recipes, look it up in this section.

Agar-agar flakes—This odorless, tasteless, and colorless sea vegetable is used as a jelling agent in desserts, aspics, jams, etc. It comes in bar, powder, and flake form. In these recipes, we use flakes.

Amasake—Literally, "sweet sake," amasake is made from rice that has been inoculated with koji (a special bacterium) and allowed to ferment for several hours. It becomes delectably sweet and creamy when it ferments, and may be purchased in several flavors. Amasake is used in making desserts, or may be enjoyed as a thick drink on its own.

Arame—This is a mild-flavored, quick-cooking sea vegetable. Rinsed and soaked for five minutes, the black strands of a small handful of arame will add an exotic note to vegetable stir-fries and other dishes. Like any sea vegetable, arame is rich in minerals, including calcium, iron, phosphorus, potassium, and iodine.

Arrowroot—The tuberus root of a tropical plant, arrowroot is dried and ground into a fine powder and used as a thickener. It may be substituted for cornstarch, measure for measure. Many health-conscious cooks prefer arrowroot to cornstarch because it is produced by a fairly simple, traditional method, whereas cornstarch is chemically bleached and treated.

Balsamic vinegar—*See* Vinegar.

Barley flour—Lightly pearled barley is ground into a flour that is wonderful in cakes, cookies, muffins, and quick breads. It gives a deliciously light and moist texture, combining beautifully with wheat flour.

Braggs Liquid Aminos—This is the brand name for a brown, liquid seasoning that is made mostly from soybeans. It can be used as a substitute for tamari or soy sauce. The flavor is somewhat different, and it does not color the dish to which it is added as much as tamari. Liquid aminos are not fermented like tamari.

Brown rice—Rice is a staple for more than half the Earth's people. Brown rice is the whole rice kernel from which only the edible hull has been removed. The bran layer is left intact, making brown rice higher in fiber, vitamins, and minerals than white rice. Because the oil in brown rice is in the surface bran layers, the rice should be stored in a cool, dry place (preferably under refrigeration).

There are several types of brown rice from which to choose, and they are all wonderful; however, in this book we use long-grain brown rice and basmati brown rice. Basmati, an aromatic rice that originated in India, is named after the tropical basmati blossom of Southeast Asia. It literally means "queen of fragrence," and basmati rice is especially fragrant. Both types of rice cook to a firm, fluffy texture, and the grains remain separate.

Carob—Although carob does not taste exactly like chocolate, it is often used as a substitute. It contains less fat than chocolate and no caffeine. Because of its natural sweetness (unlike chocolate's natural bitterness), less sweetener is needed when carob is used in place of chocolate in a recipe. But carob is an excellent food in its own right. The rich brown powder comes from grinding the dried pods of a Mediterranean locust tree. These pods are sometimes known as "St. John's Bread."

The recipes in this book call for carob chips. Make sure to read the chip ingredients and buy carob chips that are sweetened with malt, Sucanat, dates, or other natural sweeteners, and made without dairy products or saturated fats.

Chinese five spice—A mixture of five basic spices that have been ground to a powder, Chinese five spice is used throughout southern China and Vietnam to season meats and marinades. You can make your own by blending together spices in the following quantities:

> 1 tablespoon star anise
> 1 tablespoon fagara
> 1/2 tablespoon cassia or cinnamon
> 1 tablespoon fennel seed
> 1/2 tablespoon cloves

Place all the ingredients together in a blender and grind until a powder is formed. Store in a tightly covered glass jar.

Concentrated fruit sweetener—Two or more types of fruit juice are combined and boiled down to produce this syrup. Concentrated fruit sweetener can be substituted for honey in recipes; however, the results will not be quite as sweet. Honey can be substituted for concentrated fruit sweetener, with sweeter results.

Date sugar—This natural sweetener is made by simply grinding dried dates to a consistency similar to that of coarse brown sugar. Less sweet than Sucanat or honey, date sugar gives a rich moistness to baked goods.

Egg replacer—Vegetarian egg replacer is a white powder made from potato starch, tapioca flour, leavening, and carbohydrate gum. It contains no fat and is mixed with water or other liquid to use in recipes as a substitute for eggs.

Herbes de Provence—A beautiful mixture of herbs that grow plentifully in the South of France, herbes de Provence can be purchased in gourmet stores. You can also make your own by combining dried herbs in the following quantities:

3 tablespoons thyme
3 tablespoons marjoram
3 tablespoons summer savory
1 tablespoon basil
2 teaspoons rosemary
1/2 teaspoon rubbed sage
1/2 teaspoon fennel seeds

Mix well and store in a tightly covered glass jar. Use in any recipe that calls for herbs de Provence.

Liquid smoke—Made by distilling the smoke from burning hickory wood, it is highly flavored; a little goes a long way. It is not harmful to health because the distilling process filters out any carcinogens that might be in the smoke. Liquid smoke may be purchased in grocery stores.

Mirin—A sweet Japanese cooking wine made from rice, mirin can be used to flavor sauces, marinades, and desserts.

Miso—A savory fermented paste, miso imparts concentrated flavor to soups, sauces, and other foods. It is made from soybeans and/or grains, sea salt, and koji. High in sodium, miso is usually eaten in small quantities.

The numerous varieties of miso—commonly made from rice, barley, or soybeans—range from sweet white or yellow through savory reds to a dark and pungent chocolate brown. Yellow or white miso is used in this book. These types are mild and do not alter the color of foods with which they are mixed. They are especially nice for seasoning, cream soups, and mock dairy dishes.

Mochi—A traditional Japanese confection made from sweet rice, mochi is made by cooking and then pounding the rice until it becomes very smooth and sticky. This paste is spread out into slabs and allowed to partially dry. Mochi can be purchased in most natural foods stores, where it is usually kept in the frozen foods section. Cook mochi by pan-frying, baking, or grilling. As the mochi cooks, it puffs up impressively. It is crisp and crunchy on the outside and sticky and moist on the inside.

Natto miso—Sometimes called "natto miso chutney," this is a deliciously sweet and salty condiment made from barley, soybeans, koji, kombu, sea salt, and ginger. Since the fermentation time for natto miso is shorter than that for other types of miso, the grains and strips of kombu that it contains are still whole and not broken down into a paste. Natto miso is usually served alongside salads or other dishes. It can also be lightly spread over bread for use in sandwiches or added to stir-fries and grain dishes.

Nutritional yeast—*See* yeast.

Oils—Look for oils that have been mechanically extracted by low heat; they're usually labeled "unrefined" and are of the best quality. Cheaper oils, processed in huge quantities, are extracted by chemical solvents and/or very high heat. Avoid oils that are odorless, flavorless, and colorless; they have been highly filtered, bleached, and chemically treated.

For grilling most vegetables, a good olive oil is excellent. For dishes, such as desserts, where the strong flavor of olive oil is not desirable or where it would be lost in the flavor of the dish, such as curry or chili dishes, use an oil that is naturally mild-flavored, such as sunflower, safflower, or canola. Toasted sesame oil is made from toasted sesame seeds. It is used in small quantities as a seasoning.

Pink peppercorns—Available in gourmet and natural foods stores, these peppercorns have a distinctive taste. Do not substitute other types of pepper.

Quinoa—A small, hearty, disc-shaped grain, brown to gold in color, quinoa is one of the finest sources of protein in the entire vegetable kingdom. It has an almost ideal balance of amino acids along with a good complement of calcium, phosphorus, iron, B vitamins, and vitamin E. Cooked, it remains granular rather than becoming mushy and has an appealing nutty taste.

Rice Dream Beverage—This is the brand name of a white, mild-flavored beverage with a consistency similar to skim milk. Made from organic brown rice, safflower oil, and sea salt, Rice Dream is delicious on cereals or in smoothies. It may be used in some recipes to replace soy or dairy milk, but it tends to curdle when heated, which makes it undesirable for some dishes. (In our pie recipe on page 203, Rice Dream works beautifully because it is blended *after* it is cooked.)

Rice vinegar—*See* Vinegar.

Seitan—A meat analog made from wheat gluten, a natural protein, seitan is basically wheat flour with the starch removed.

To make seitan, gluten dough is slowly simmered in a flavored broth until it becomes firm and chewy. Prepared seitan can be purchased in the refrigerator section of most large natural foods stores. It usually comes with a broth that can either be used or discarded.

Sesame butter—*See* Tahini, sesame.

Silken tofu—*See* Tofu.

Sesame oil, toasted—*See* Oil.

Shoyu—*See* Tamari.

Soy cheese—This nondairy cheese substitute is made mostly from soy milk. Most soy cheeses contain the milk derivative casein, but there is a brand without it (Vegan Rella). The trick to using soy cheese successfully in recipes is to use it lightly. Too much soy cheese in a recipe does not taste as good as a light sprinkling of it.

Sucanat—This sweetener is made from the juice of organically grown sugar cane that has been dehydrated to form a powder with the taste and consistency of brown sugar. Unlike refined sugar, Sucanat is a whole food. It is not quite as sweet as brown sugar or honey, but it is sweeter than date sugar or fruit concentrate. Sucanat is excellent for making cakes and cookies. Substitute Sucanat for brown sugar, measure for measure, in any recipe.

Sun-dried tomato halves—The sun-dried tomatoes called for in this book are not preserved in oil, making them lower in fat and less expensive. Use dried tomato halves that are sold in cellophane bags (I use the Sonoma brand found in natural foods stores).

Tahini, sesame—This is a raw purée of hulled sesame seeds. Tahini can be used in Middle Eastern dishes, meatless loaves and burgers, spreads, sauces, and desserts. Sesame butter, made from toasted sesame seeds, has a stronger, richer flavor than tahini. The two can be used interchangeably.

Tamari—Also called wheat-free tamari, this natural Japanese soy sauce has a dark color and rich flavor. Shoyu (which is often misnamed "tamari") contains wheat but otherwise is similar to tamari. The two can be used interchangeably. Both tamari and shoyu are fermented in wooden kegs for as long as two years. The cheap mass-market soy sauces can in no way compare with the fine flavor of the real thing.

Teff—A tiny brown seed of Ethiopian origin, teff is now grown in North Dakota. The smallest grain, it is high in protein and quite versatile. Uncooked, teff can be added to many baked goods or substituted for part of the seeds, nuts, or small grains called for in a recipe. Cooked teff (one part teff in three parts water, simmered for fifteen minutes) is gelatinous and adds body to puddings and refrigerator pies. It is an excellent thickener for soups, stews, and gravies. Its mild, slightly molasses-like sweetness makes teff easy to use.

Tempeh—A traditional food from Indonesia, tempeh is made from partially cooked, split, and hulled soybeans that are inoculated with a special bacterium and incubated for about twenty-four hours. During the incubation, a white, fluffy mold develops around the beans, holding them together in a slab. Tempeh has a firm but tender texture and is very pleasant. It is high in protein and easy to digest.

The only drawback to tempeh is that it is very perishable and must be used or frozen within a few days after it is made. Unlike tofu, tempeh must be cooked before it is eaten. Cook tempeh by pan-frying, broiling, grilling, or steaming.

Tofu—A staple of both Chinese and Japanese cuisines, tofu has become very popular in the West in recent years. It is high in protein, low in calories, rich in calcium, easy to digest, and convenient to use. Tofu can be transformed into an amazing variety of scrumptious dishes, from protein-rich entries to creamy desserts. If you tried tofu and found it unappealing, try it on the grill and see if you don't change your mind.

Tofu is made by soaking whole soybeans for eight to ten hours, then grinding them into a purée. This purée is pressed through a cloth to extract the soy milk from the pulp. The milk is cooked and a coagulant (traditionally nigari, which is extracted from sea salt) is added to curdle it. The curds are carefully ladled into a mold, where they are pressed until firm. The resulting tofu is stored in cold water.

It is not necessary to make your own tofu; delicious tofu, in two textures—soft and firm—is available in the produce section at supermarkets and in natural foods stores. When refrigerated, tofu will keep for a week or more. Unless the tofu you purchase is in a sealed container, it must be kept immersed in water. Change this water daily to keep it fresh. Old tofu develops an unpleasant, sour odor. Very fresh tofu is especially mild and sweet.

If a recipe calls for tofu, do not use silken tofu, a very soft and custard-like tofu coagulated with calcium sulfate rather than nigari. It is sold in cardboard containers and does not have to be refrigerated until it is opened. Silken tofu comes in three textures. It is milder in flavor than regular tofu and is used in many recipes for sauces and for desserts.

If a recipe calls for silken tofu, do not use regular tofu. Make sure to notice whether the recipe calls for firm, soft, or extra firm tofu, and use the kind indicated in the recipe.

Tofu parmesan—A dairy analog, this tofu product tastes and looks a lot like Parmesan cheese. Use it anywhere you would use grated parmesan. Beware, however, that there are minute quantities of casein (which is a milk derivative) in almost all soy cheese.

TVP (textured vegetable protein)—This high-protein convenience food is made from soybeans. It is quick and easy to use. Added to spaghetti sauces, chili, veggie burgers, etc., it imparts the texture of ground meat along with its protein boost.

Vinegar—The word "vinegar" comes from the French words *vin* (wine) and *aigre* (sour) and the substance has been used for thousands of years. Rice vinegar is made from fermented rice; cider vinegar, from apple juice; wine vinegar, from red or white wine; and balsamic vinegar, from sweet wine. Although each has its own special flavor and aroma, different vinegars can be used interchangeably in most recipes, with the exception of umeboshi vinegar (a Japanese vinegar made from a salt-pickled plum). Umeboshi vinegar is salty as well as sour. If you wish to substitute another vinegar for umeboshi vinegar, use wine or cider vinegar and then increase the salt in the recipe to taste.

Vital wheat gluten—Wheat gluten is the natural protein derived from wheat. The addition of gluten to your bread dough will produce consistent, uniform, well-risen loaves. We use Arrowhead Mills Vital Wheat Gluten, which is extracted from wheat through a water-washing procedure. The process is entirely mechanical with no chemicals used or added. Vital wheat gluten is higher in gluten than gluten flour, which is refined wheat flour with some gluten mixed in.

Whole-grain pasta—There are many varieties of whole-grain pasta available in natural foods stores. Some varieties are better for both taste and nutrition than others. Some of the pastas sold in natural foods stores taste good, but are made from unbleached white flour with the addition of herbs or vegetable coloring to make them appear natural. On the other hand, there are whole-grain pastas made from organic flour that are thick and pasty. However, there are nutritious whole-grain pastas whose taste can compete with the less nutritious refined varieties.

Spelt pasta is usually very good, as is quinoa pasta. For persons with wheat allergies, there are pastas made from corn and rice. Some of these are quite good. If you try a whole-grain pasta and are not satisfied with it, try another variety the next time. We're sure that you will find one that you like.

Whole-wheat bread flour—This high-gluten flour is made from hard red wheat. Because of its high gluten content, it is the best flour to use when making yeast breads.

Whole-wheat pastry flour—Made from soft wheat, it is lower in gluten and has a lighter consistency than whole-wheat bread flour. It is preferable for making pastries, cakes, cookies, and similar baked goods.

Yeast, dry active—Used for leavening, dry active yeast is composed of dormant living microorganisms. Moisture and warmth activate them. Fresh cake yeast may be substituted for dry active yeast, tablespoon for tablespoon. Inactive food yeasts, such as torula, brewer's, and nutritional yeast, have no leavening power.

Yeast, nutritional—An excellent food supplement, nutritional yeast is very rich in B vitamins and protein, but low in calories. Like all other yeasts, nutritional yeast is composed of microorganisms; unlike those other yeasts, however, these microorganisms are inactive and safe to eat without cooking. Nutritional yeast has a mild cheese-like or nutty flavor. Don't confuse it with brewer's yeast or torula yeast, both of which taste terrible, or with dry active yeast or fresh cake yeast, which will cause great discomfort if eaten raw.

Used in your daily cooking, nutritional yeast adds flavor and nutrients to soups, sauces, stews, mock-meat dishes, and salads. It is surprisingly good sprinkled over green salad.

Appetizers

An appetizer should whet the appetite. We think you'll find that the following treats will leave you wanting to eat, eat, eat.

Our pâtés all contain grilled ingredients. The grilling gives them a hearty, robust flavor that can compete with any pâté de fois gras, without the high fat and cholesterol. Serve pâtés with crusty whole-grain bread or crackers for an appetizer, or feature them along with soup or salad. For a gourmet lunch, try vegetarian pâtés in sandwiches with lettuce, tomato, and mustard.

We've also included recipes for grilled mochi, polenta, and ratatouille, as well as the traditional appetizing favorites, stuffed mushrooms and antipasto.

Hestia's Pâté

Hestia was the goddess of home and hearth.
One of her main jobs was to keep the hearth fires
burning. Had she lived close to the Orient,
she might have used those fires to add a delicate
smoked taste to tempeh. What better use for
this delicacy than a rich-tasting pâté?

Yield: 8 servings (about 2 1/2 cups)
Time: 15 minutes to prepare
15–18 minutes to cook

1/2 pound tempeh, thawed if frozen
water sufficient to steam tempeh
2 tablespoons oil
2 tablespoons tamari
1 teaspoon liquid smoke
3 cups sliced mushrooms
1–2 cloves garlic, pressed
1/2 teaspoon thyme
1/2 teaspoon sage
2 tablespoons tahini
3 tablespoons water

1. Cut the tempeh into bite-sized pieces and place them in a vegetable steamer. Place the vegetable steamer in a pan with a little water in the bottom. Cover the pan and bring the water to a boil. Reduce the heat and steam the tempeh for about 10 minutes.

2. In a mixing bowl, combine the oil, tamari, and liquid smoke. Mix well. Add the steamed tempeh and mix again to coat the tempeh. Place a rack with small holes on the bottom rack of your grill. Using a slotted spoon, remove the tempeh from the liquid and place it on the rack. Cook over low heat, turning

often, until the tempeh is well browned (2–5 minutes). Place it in a food processor.

3. Place the mushrooms in the bowl in which the tempeh was mixed. Stir to coat them with any remaining oil mixture (if there is not much, don't worry). Place the mushrooms on the grill and cook, stirring often, until they are done (about 5–8 minutes).

4. Place the mushrooms in the food processor with the tempeh. Add the remaining ingredients and blend until smooth.

5. Serve this pâté warm or cold.

Serving Suggestion

Hestia's Pâté makes delicious sandwiches with mustard, lettuce, and tomato.

🍂 *BARBECUE TIDBIT* 🍂

To add more smoke flavor to grilled foods, use wood chips from a variety of hardwoods or fruit woods. Such chips can be purchased at stores that sell barbecue supplies. To use these wood chips, first soak them in water, and then place them in a packet of aluminum foil. Poke some holes in the foil and lay the packet between the charcoals or beside the lava rocks. Do not place the chips directly on the rocks because there will be much too much smoke. ❑

Titania's Tapinade

*Titania, that queen of pleasure immortalized
in Shakespeare's Midsummer Night's Dream, would have
loved tapinade—a black olive and anchovy spread that is
served in the South of France. We've substituted grilled
onions for the anchovies, and we really like the results.*

Yield: 8 servings (about 2 cups)
Time: About 5 minutes to prepare
About 5 minutes to cook

*2 cups coarsely chopped onions
1 tablespoon olive oil
1 can (drained weight 6 ounces)
pitted black olives
1 teaspoon thyme
1/4 teaspoon salt*

1. Place the onions in a mixing bowl. Add the oil and mix well.
    Place a rack with small holes on the bottom rack of your grill.
    Place the onions on the rack and cook over low heat, stirring
    often, until they are tender (about 5 minutes).

2. Combine the grilled onions, drained olives, thyme, and salt in
    a food processor. Blend until smooth. Scrape the sides of the
    food processor with a rubber spatula if necessary to make sure
    the spread gets well blended.

3. Chill before serving.

Serving Suggestion

Serve with whole-grain crackers or bread.

Pâté Olympus

The gods who lived on Mt. Olympus were a sensuous lot—eating ambrosia, drinking nectar, and having liasons with scores of mortals. This delicious and easy spread would have been a favorite of theirs as mushrooms, a highly prized delicacy associated with Mother Earth, were considered a food of the gods.

Yield: 8 servings (approximately 2 cups)

Time: 15 minutes to prepare

15 minutes to grill

1 medium eggplant (about 1 pound)
1 tablespoon olive oil
3 1/2 cups sliced mushrooms
1 tablespoon olive oil
8–10 cloves garlic
1 teaspoon oregano
1 teaspoon basil
2 tablespoons tamari

1. Wash the eggplant and cut into 1/2-inch-thick slices. Brush the eggplant slices with 1 tablespoon of oil. Place the eggplant slices on the grill and cook over low heat for about 5 minutes or until they are brown on the bottom. Turn them over and cook until they are brown on the other side. Set aside.

2. In a mixing bowl, combine the sliced mushrooms and the remaining tablespoon of oil. Mix well to coat the mushrooms with the oil. Place the rack with small holes over the bottom rack of your grill and cook the mushrooms, stirring often, until they are done (about 5 minutes).

3. Remove the skin from the garlic cloves. Place a rack with small holes on the top rack of the grill. Place a small sheet of heavy-duty aluminum foil on the rack and roast the garlic cloves over low heat until they are brown and tender. Turn them often to keep them from burning.

4. In a food processor, combine the roasted eggplant, mush-

rooms, garlic, herbs, and tamari. Blend until smooth. Stop the
food processor once or twice during the operation and scrape
the sides with a rubber spatula to make sure that the pâté gets
well blended. If necessary, blend the pâté in two batches.

5. Serve warm or cold.

Serving Suggestion

Pâté Olympus is wonderful with whole-grain bread or crackers
and sliced ripe tomatoes.

Apollo's Antipasto

*The rich colors of this antipasto, the juicy tomatoes,
and the spicy vegetable pepperoni are truly splendid.
Who other than Apollo could give his name to this
beautiful way to put together leftovers.*

Yield: Servings will vary

Time: About 5 minutes

Bathsheba Eggplant (page 109)
Swashbuckler Salad (page 61)
or roasted bell peppers
Zucchini à la Bacchus (page 104)
1 large ripe tomato, sliced
Yves Veggie Pepperoni, sliced

1. On a serving platter, arrange slices of Bathsheba Eggplant,
   roasted bell peppers or Swashbuckler Salad, Zucchini à la Bacchus, slices of ripe tomato, and slices of Yves Veggie Pepperoni.

Serving Suggestion

Serve Apollo's Antipasto with Reveler's Relish (page 84) and
Focaccia (page 91).

Catherine Deneuve's Pâté

*This tofu pâté tastes a lot like the meat pâté
that is served in France, or so we were told
by Vicki's French husband.*

Yield: 8 servings
Time: 20 minutes to prepare
20 minutes to grill
3 hours to chill

1 teaspoon liquid smoke
1 tablespoon tamari
1 tablespoon oil
1 pound firm tofu, cut into 1-inch cubes
2 cups chopped onions
1 tablespoon oil
1 cup water
3 tablespoons tamari
1 tablespoon agar-agar flakes
1/2 teaspoon sage
1 teaspoon thyme

1. In a mixing bowl, combine the liquid smoke, 1 tablespoon tamari, and 1 tablespoon oil. Add the tofu and mix well. Place a rack with small holes on the bottom rack of the grill. Place the tofu on the grill and cook it over low heat, turning often, until it is browned on all sides (about 10–12 minutes). Place the grilled tofu in a food processor.

2. In a mixing bowl, combine the onions with the remaining tablespoon of oil. Mix well. Place the onions on the grill and cook over low heat, stirring often, until they are tender (5–10 minutes).

3. Add the onions to the tofu in the food processor. Blend to grind the tofu and the onions. Set aside.

4. In a saucepan, combine the water, tamari, agar-agar flakes,

sage, and thyme. Bring the mixture to a boil. Cover and reduce the heat. Cook over low heat, stirring occasionally, until the agar is dissolved (about 10 minutes).

5. When the agar is dissolved, pour the hot liquid into the food processor with the tofu and onions. Blend until smooth.

6. Rinse a medium-sized bowl or a loaf pan in cold water. Pour the hot mixture into the pan or bowl. Refrigerate until firm (about 3 hours).

7. To serve, run a knife around the edges of the pâté and invert the mold over a serving plate. Garnish with parsley and black olives.

Serving Suggestion

This pâté slices beautifully. It is delicious with bread or crackers as an appetizer, or in sandwiches with mustard and lettuce, or sprouts and tomato.

Mochi

*Mochi is a traditional Japanese confection
made from sweet rice.*

Yield: 4 servings

Time: About 10 minutes to grill

*1 package (8 1/2 ounces) mochi (any flavor)
1 teaspoon oil*

1. Break the mochi into pieces where it is scored. Brush it lightly
    with oil.

2. Place the mochi on the bottom rack of the grill and cook over
    low heat for 3–4 minutes or until it is brown on the bottom.
    (Move the mochi around on the grill as it cooks so that it
    doesn't burn.) Turn it over and cook until it puffs up (about
    4–5 minutes more).

Serving Suggestion

Mochi is delicious for breakfast or brunch with Fruit de Soma
(page 186). It makes an easy dessert or sweet treat with honey or
maple syrup, or you can spread it with peanut or almond butter.
Garlic-flavored mochi, which is available commercially, can be
served in place of bread with soup or salad.

Babette's Feast

*A sizzling riot of colors and rich tastes,
our ratatouille is an aromatic delight as well.*

Yield: 4–6 servings
Time: 15 minutes for eggplant to drain
30 minutes to prepare
20 minutes to grill

1 large eggplant
1/2 teaspoon sea salt
1 tablespoon olive oil
1 medium zucchini, sliced
1 medium yellow squash, sliced
1 large green pepper
2 cups small, whole mushrooms
2 tablespoons olive oil, divided
1 cup chopped onion
3 bay leaves
1 teaspoon basil
1/2 teaspoon oregano
*1 can tomato purée (28 ounces) or 3 medium
tomatoes, blended in a blender*
*20 sun-dried tomato halves,
cut into small pieces with a scissors*

1. Cut the eggplant into 1/2-inch-thick slices. Lightly sprinkle the slices with sea salt, stack them, and let them sit in a shallow dish for about 15 minutes.

2. Rinse and dry the eggplant. Lightly brush the eggplant slices with 1 tablespoon of oil. Place a rack with small holes on the bottom rack of your grill and cook the eggplant slices over low heat until they are brown on the bottom. Turn them over and

cook until they are tender (about 10 minutes in all). Set aside for later use.

3. Place the sliced zucchini, squash, green pepper, and mushrooms together in a large bowl. Add 1 tablespoon of oil and mix well. Place the vegetables on the grill and cook, stirring often, until tender (about 10 minutes). Remove the vegetables from the heat and let sit while you make the sauce.

4. In a large kettle, heat the remaining tablespoon oil. Add the onion, bay leaves, basil, and oregano. Sauté over medium heat for about 5 minutes. Add the tomato purée and the sun-dried tomato pieces. Simmer, uncovered, over low heat for about 10 minutes.

5. Cut the grilled eggplant into cubes and add to the sauce along with the other grilled vegetables. Let simmer for about 5 minutes to blend the flavors.

Serving Suggestion

Serve over whole-grain pasta or over brown rice. Accompany with a big green salad.

Marcello's Mushrooms

These stuffed mushrooms, pungent and earthy, make us think of those ever-famous Italian lovers. Mama Mia!

Yield: 5 servings
Time: 15 minutes to prepare
15 minutes to grill

10 very large mushrooms (1 pound)
2 tablespoons olive oil
2 tablespoons minced garlic
1 teaspoon herbes de Provence
1 cup whole-grain bread crumbs
1/4 cup TVP
1 tablespoon tamari
2 tablespoons minced parsley

1. Wash and dry the mushrooms. Cut off the stems and chop them into small pieces. Reserve the tops.

2. Heat the olive oil in a skillet. Add the garlic and herbs. Sauté for 1–2 minutes then add the chopped mushroom stems. Sauté for about 2 minutes more or until the stems are cooked Add the bread crumbs, TVP, and tamari. Mix well. Stuff the mushroom tops with this mixture.

3. Place the stuffed mushrooms in an oiled metal cake pan (an 8-inch x 8-inch pan works well). Cover the pan with a piece of aluminum foil and place it on the top rack of the grill. Cook over medium-low heat for about 10 minutes.

4. Remove the mushrooms from the pan and carefully place them on the bottom rack of the grill. Let them cook for about 3–5 minutes more or until they are grilled on the bottom.

5. Before serving, sprinkle the mushrooms with parsley.

Soups

In these soups, the vegetables are first grilled and then added to the soup stock. They are not the quickest soups to make, but our guests have repeatedly assured us that they are worth the effort. They can be made in advance and heated before serving.

With some veggie pâté, a loaf of crusty whole-grain bread, and a nice green salad, any of these soups can make a delicious, nutritious, and satisfying meal.

Scarlet Pimpernel Pot

*Delicately flavored with a rich creamy texture
and beautiful color, this roasted red-pepper cream
can be served either hot or cold.*

Yield: 4–6 servings
Time: 25 minutes to prepare
30 minutes to cook
(add 2–3 hours chilling time if soup is served cold)

*1 tablespoon olive oil
1 Spanish onion, chopped (3 cups)
6 medium red bell peppers
2 cups water
1/2 cup cashews
2 cups water
2 tablespoons white miso
1 teaspoon sea salt
1 tablespoon balsamic vinegar
1 tablespoon mirin
2 tablespoons fresh chives*

1. Heat the oil in a large skillet or Dutch oven. Add the onion and sauté very slowly over low heat for 20–30 minutes. Stir occasionally.

2. While the onion is cooking, roast the peppers. Place them on the bottom rack of your grill over low heat and cook, turning often, until they are charred and blistered all over (10–15 minutes).

3. Place the peppers in a paper bag (or a bowl with a dish towel over the top), and let them cool for about 15 minutes or until you can handle them without burning yourself.

4. Place 2 cups of the water in a blender. Add the cashews and

blend until creamy. Add the cashew cream to the onion. Bring the mixture to a boil while stirring constantly. Reduce the heat and simmer for 3–4 minutes.

5. Put the cashew mixture in the blender and blend until very smooth and creamy. Pour the mixture into a bowl if the soup is to be served cold or into a kettle if the soup is to be served hot.

6. When the peppers are cool, cut them in half and remove the seeds and stems. Using your hands, peel the skin off the peppers.

7. Place the peppers in the blender with the remaining water. Add the miso, salt, vinegar, and mirin. Blend. Add this mixture to the cashew mixture and stir.

8. If the soup is to be eaten hot, stir it over medium heat until it is hot but do not bring to a boil. If the soup is to be eaten cold, place it in the refrigerator to cool for 2–3 hours. Add the chives just before serving.

Serving Suggestion

Two tablespoons of finely chopped fresh basil may be used in addition to or in place of the chives.

Salome's Tomato and White Bean Soup

Soup is such simple yet hearty fare!

Yield: 8 servings

Time: About 35 minutes to prepare

About 30 minutes to cook

---

1 tablespoon olive oil

1 1/2 cups chopped onion

1 cup finely chopped celery

1 teaspoon oregano

1 teaspoon basil

3 bay leaves

*2 cans (15 ounces each) great northern beans,
with liquid*

2 1/2 pounds ripe red tomatoes

*1 1/2 pounds ripe yellow tomatoes
(If yellow tomatoes are not available,
substitute red tomatoes.)*

*1 pound Italian plum tomatoes,
quartered*

1 tablespoon olive oil

2 Belgian endives, cut into halves lengthwise

1 teaspoon olive oil

3 cloves garlic, pressed

1 teaspoon sea salt

1/2 cup water

1. In a large, heavy kettle heat 1 tablespoon olive oil. Add the onion, celery, oregano, basil, and bay leaves. Sauté until the onions and celery are tender (about 10 minutes). Add the beans with their liquid (do not drain) and set aside.

2. Slice the red tomatoes in 1/2–3/4-inch-thick slices and place them on the bottom rack of the grill over medium-low heat. Cook for 3–4 minutes or until they are grilled on the bottom. Turn them over and grill on the other side. Remove the tomatoes from the heat and place them in a blender. Blend until smooth and add the purée to the kettle with the beans.

3. Repeat step 2 using the yellow tomatoes but do not blend. Chop them and add them to the kettle.

4. Place a rack with small holes on the bottom rack of the grill. Brush the plum tomatoes with 1 tablespoon of olive oil and grill for about 3–5 minutes. Add them to the kettle.

5. Brush the endives with 1 teaspoon of olive oil and place them on the grill, cut side down. Cook until they are browned on the bottom (3–4 minutes), then turn them over and cook 2–3 minutes more. Transfer the endives to a cutting board and coarsely chop them. Add them to the soup.

6. Bring the soup to a simmer and let it cook for about 5 minutes to blend the flavors. Add the garlic, salt, and water. Mix well and serve.

Serving Suggestion

This soup makes a meal when served with whole-grain bread and a big green salad.

Sheba's Soup

King Solomon was more than willing to sing
for his supper when the Queen of Sheba served
this colorful and flavorful soup.

Yield: 6 servings
Time: About 30 minutes to prepare
About 20 minutes to cook

1 1/2 tablespoons olive oil
2 tablespoons tamari
4 cloves garlic
3 tablespoons mirin
2 cups coarsely chopped onions
2 cups carrots (2 medium)
cut into match-stick shapes
2 small yellow squash, diced
1 green pepper, diced
2 cups corn, cut off the cob
1 large can (28 ounces) tomatoes
3 cups water
1 teaspoon sea salt
2 tablespoons fresh basil

1. In a large mixing bowl, combine the olive oil, tamari, garlic, and mirin. Mix well. Add the onions. Mix again to coat the onions.

2. Place a rack with small holes over the bottom rack of your grill. Remove the onions from the tamari mixture with a slotted spoon and place them on the grill over low heat. Cook, stirring often. When the onions are tender (2–3 minutes), transfer them to a large kettle and set aside.

3. Place the carrots in the bowl in which you mixed the onions. Mix well to coat with the remaining tamari mixture. Remove the carrots from the bowl with a slotted spoon and place them

on the rack. Cook over low heat, turning often, until the carrots are tender (3–4 minutes). Transfer them to the kettle with the onions.

4. Repeat step 2 using the yellow squash first, then the pepper.

5. When all the vegetables are grilled, add the can of tomatoes, corn, water, and salt to the kettle. Bring the mixture to a boil. Reduce the heat and simmer for about 10 minutes to blend the flavors.

6. Add the fresh basil just before serving.

Lady Chatterly's Chowder

Enjoy spicy corn chowder with a pretty golden color and the added flavor of grilled vegetables.

Yield: 4–6 servings
Time: About 20 minutes to prepare
About 20 minutes to cook

1 pound new potatoes
2 medium yellow zucchini
2 tablespoons oil, divided
1 1/2 cups chopped onion
corn cut from 3 cobs
1 1/2 cups water
2 cups soy milk
1 teaspoon sea salt
1 teaspoon cumin
1/4 teaspoon turmeric
1/2 teaspoon paprika
pinch of cayenne, if desired

1. Scrub the potatoes and cut out any bad spots. Cut them into
    3/4-inch cubes. Steam or pressure cook until the cubes are just
    barely tender. Place 1/2 cup of the potatoes in a blender or food
    processor. Place the remaining potatoes in a mixing bowl.

2. Cut the zucchini in cubes that are about the same size as the
    potato cubes and place them in the bowl. Add 1 tablespoon of
    the oil and mix gently. Place a rack with small holes on the
    bottom rack of your grill and transfer the vegetables to the
    rack. Cook over medium heat, turning frequently with a spat-
    ula, until the potatoes are nicely browned and the zucchini is
    tender (about 5 minutes). Return the vegetables to the bowl.

3. Heat the remaining tablespoon of oil in a large, heavy kettle.
    Add the onion and sauté until tender.

4. While the onion is cooking, place 1 cup of corn in the blender
    with the potatoes. Add 1 cup of water and blend until smooth
    and creamy. Add this mixture to the sautéed onions. Add the
    remaining corn and the remaining 1/2 cup water. Bring the
    mixture to a boil while stirring often. Reduce the heat and
    simmer for 3–5 minutes.

5. Add the grilled vegetables, soy milk, salt, cumin, turmeric,
    and paprika. Mix well. Bring the soup back to a simmer, and
    let it cook over low heat for 5–10 minutes, stirring occasion-
    ally. Taste the soup and add a pinch of cayenne, if desired.

Three-Musketeer Soup

*Combine mushrooms, "cream," and herbs
and you've a trio that you'll never want to split!
Grilling the mushrooms gives this soup a flavor
and texture that reminds us of the wild mushroom soups
that we make in France.*

Yield: 4 servings
Time: About 20 minutes to prepare
About 25 minutes to cook

1 tablespoon oil

1 1/3 cups finely chopped celery

1 cup finely chopped onion

3 tablespoons whole-wheat pastry flour

4 cups soy milk

*1 tablespoon finely chopped fresh basil
(or 1 teaspoon dry)*

*2 teaspoons finely chopped fresh rosemary
(or 1 teaspoon dry)*

1 teaspoon thyme

1 teaspoon oregano

2 tablespoons Braggs Liquid Aminos

*1 pound mushrooms,
cleaned and cut into bite-sized pieces*

1 tablespoon oil

1. Heat 1 tablespoon oil in a large, heavy kettle. Add the celery and onion. Sauté over low heat until both the celery and the onion are tender (about 10 minutes).

2. Sprinkle about 1/2 of the flour over the sautéed vegetables. Mix well and sprinkle in the rest of the flour. Mix well. Stir over medium heat to brown the flour. While stirring constantly over medium-high heat, gradually add the milk. Add

the herbs and the Braggs and simmer until the soup is thick. Set aside.

3. Place the mushrooms in a mixing bowl. Drizzle the remaining tablespoon of oil over them and mix well. Place a rack with small holes on the bottom rack of your grill. Transfer the mushrooms to the rack. Cook over medium-low heat for 5–10 minutes, or until the mushrooms are browned and reduced in size. Turn them often as they cook.

4. Add the mushrooms to the soup. Mix and simmer for 2–3 minutes. If the soup becomes too thick, add a little soy milk.

Chisum Chili

*If you really want to spice up your love life,
here's the dish that will do it. Even meat-lovers will enjoy
this spicy vegetarian chili.*

Yield: 6 servings
Time: Soak beans overnight
About 40 minutes to prepare
1–2 hours to cook

1 cup dry kidney beans

3 cups water

*16-ounce jar seitan,
drained and cut into bite-sized pieces*

1 tablespoon olive oil

1 teaspoon liquid smoke

2 cups chopped onions

1 teaspoon olive oil

1 green bell pepper, diced

1 red pepper, diced

1 teaspoon olive oil

16-ounce can tomatoes

4 cloves garlic, pressed

1 1/2 tablespoons balsamic vinegar

1 teaspoon basil

1/2 teaspoon oregano

1 teaspoon cumin

1 tablespoon chili powder

1/2–1 jalapeño pepper, minced

1/2–1 teaspoon sea salt, to taste

1. Wash and pick through the beans, discarding any dirt or small stones. Place the beans in a bowl and cover them with about 1 1/2 inches of water. Let soak for 8–10 hours.

2. Drain and rinse the beans. Place them in a large kettle with 3 cups of water. Cover and bring to a boil. Reduce the heat and simmer, stirring occasionally, until the beans are tender (1–2 hours).

3. Place the seitan in a bowl with 1 tablespoon of oil and the liquid smoke. Mix well to coat the seitan with the oil. Place a rack with small holes on the bottom rack of your grill and place the seitan on the rack over low heat. Cook, turning often, until the seitan is well browned (about 10 minutes).

4. Place the grilled seitan in a food processor and grind. Add to the cooked beans.

5. In a mixing bowl, combine the onions with 1 teaspoon of oil. Mix well. Grill until tender. Add to the kettle with the beans.

6. In a mixing bowl, combine the diced bell peppers with the remaining teaspoon of oil. Grill until tender (about 8 minutes). Add to the kettle with the beans.

7. Add the can of tomatoes, the garlic, vinegar, basil, oregano, cumin, chili powder, 1/2 of the jalapeño pepper, and the salt. Bring the mixture to a boil, reduce the heat, and simmer for about 10 minutes to blend the flavors. Taste the chili. If desired, add more salt and the other half of the jalapeño pepper.

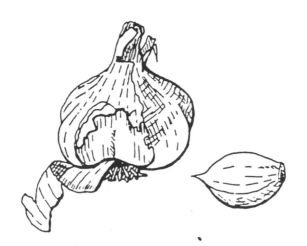

Salads

Salads made from grilled vegetables are wonderful for dinner parties and pot lucks because they can be made in advance. Grilling the vegetables in these salads makes them especially flavorful, and allows them to retain their color.

Serve salads on beds of fresh mixed greens at the beginning of a meal, or to accompany tofu, tempeh, or seitan dishes.

Penelope's Salad

*Ulysses' ever-faithful wife would have enjoyed
this grilled eggplant with its Mediterranean flavor.*

Yield: 6 servings
Time: About 10 minutes to prepare
10 minutes to cook
2–3 hours chilling time

*1 medium-large eggplant (1 1/4 pounds)
sliced into 1/2-inch-thick rounds*

2 tablespoons olive oil

1 small green bell pepper

2 medium-sized tomatoes

1 cup pitted black olive halves

2 tablespoons tamari

2 tablespoons balsamic vinegar

2 cloves garlic, pressed

*1 teaspoon finely chopped fresh rosemary
(or 1/2 teaspoon dry)*

*1 tablespoon finely chopped fresh basil
(or 1 teaspoon dry)*

1/2 cup finely chopped parsley

1. Brush the eggplant with the olive oil. Place it on the grill over low heat and cook until it is browned on the bottom (about 5 minutes). Turn it over and cook until it is browned on the other side and tender (about 5 minutes more). Set the eggplant aside to cool, and prepare the other ingredients.

2. Finely chop the green bell pepper and tomatoes.

3. Place the remaining ingredients in a large mixing bowl. When the eggplant is cool enough to handle, cut it into bite-sized cubes. Add the eggplant to the other ingredients. Mix well.

4. Chill for 2–3 hours before serving.

Serving Suggestion

Penelope's Salad is a good companion for rice dishes or protein dishes. Leftover salad makes a delicious filling for pita bread.

Salad of Eden

This easy salad has a wonderful smoked flavor

Yield: 4 servings

Time: About 5 minutes to prepare

About 5 minutes to cook

(add about 1 1/2 hours if salad is served cold)

20 cherry tomatoes, halved
2 tablespoons olive oil
2 tablespoons balsamic vinegar
2 tablespoons tamari
2 tablespoons minced fresh basil
1/4 cup minced fresh parsley

1. In a salad bowl, combine the tomatoes, oil, vinegar, and tamari. Place a rack with small holes on the bottom rack of your grill. Transfer the tomato mixture from the bowl onto the grill. *Be careful not to burn yourself;* the oil falling from the tomatoes will cause a flare-up. Cook over medium heat, turning constantly with a spatula, for 3–5 minutes.

2. Return the tomatoes to the salad bowl and add the herbs. Serve hot or cold.

Orpheus' Salad

*The famed Greek musician Orpheus descended
into Hades in search of his beloved Eurydice.
You'll hear his music when you eat this salad
redolent with the taste of Greece.*

Yield: 6–8 servings
Time: 20 minutes to prepare
About 25 minutes to cook

Salad

2 1/2 pounds new potatoes

1 tablespoon olive oil

2 cups coarsely diced onions

1 red bell pepper, diced

1 yellow bell pepper, diced

1 green bell pepper, diced

1 tablespoon olive oil

1 cucumber, diced

1 cup pitted black olives, cut into halves

1 cup pitted green olives, cut into halves

1 pint cherry tomatoes, cut into halves

Dressing

1 tablespoon olive oil

1 teaspoon basil

1 teaspoon oregano

1/2 teaspoon dill seeds

1 teaspoon sea salt

2 tablespoons balsamic vinegar

1. Scrub the potatoes—do not peel—and cut out any bad spots.
   Cut potatoes into bite-sized chunks. Steam or pressure cook
   the chunks until they are just barely tender.

2. Drain the potatoes and mix them with 1 tablespoon of olive oil. Place a rack with small holes on the bottom rack of your grill. Place the potatoes on the rack and cook over medium heat, turning often until the pootatoes are crispy brown (5–10 minutes). Set aside.

3. In a mixing bowl, combine the onions, bell peppers, and 1 tablespoon olive oil. Mix well. Grill the vegetables over low heat, stirring often, until tender (about 10 minutes). Place with the grilled potatoes and refrigerate.

4. When the vegetables are cool, add the cucumber, olives, and cherry tomatoes.

5. In a small bowl, combine all the ingredients for the dressing. Mix well and pour the dressing over the salad. Mix gently.

6. Serve immediately or return the salad to the refrigerator and serve later.

Salad à la Chloe

*What could be more simple or more earthy than
the potato? Add fines herbes and give potato salad
a French flair.*

Yield: 6 servings
Time: About 15 minutes to prepare
15–20 minutes to cook
2 hours to chill

*1 large red pepper
2 pounds new potatoes
3 tablespoons olive oil
3 tablespoons lemon juice
2 cloves garlic, pressed
2 tablespoons tamari
2 tablespoons minced fresh basil
1/4 cup minced parsley
2 tablespoons minced fresh dill*

1. Place the red pepper on the bottom rack of the grill and cook over low heat, about 10–15 minutes. Turn the pepper often until it becomes soft and blistered all over. Place the pepper in a paper bag or a bowl with a dish towel over the top and let it cool while you cook the potatoes.

2. Scrub the potatoes—do not peel—and cut them into bite-sized chunks. Steam or pressure cook until they are just barely tender. Do not over-cook.

3. Drain the potatoes and place them in a large bowl with 1 tablespoon of the oil. Mix well. Place a rack with small holes on the bottom rack of your grill. Transfer the potatoes to the rack and cook over low heat, turning often, until they are tender and nicely browned (about 5 minutes). Return the potatoes to the mixing bowl and place it in the refrigerator.

4. Cut the pepper in half, and remove the seeds and the stem.

Using your hands peel the pepper, then cut it into small strips. Place it in the bowl with the potatoes.

5. In another bowl, combine the remaining 2 tablespoons of olive oil, the lemon juice, garlic, tamari, and chopped herbs. Add this mixture to the roasted potatoes and pepper. Mix well and chill. Before serving, mix again.

Serving Suggestion

Serve on leaves of curly lettuce to appeal to the eye as well as the palate.

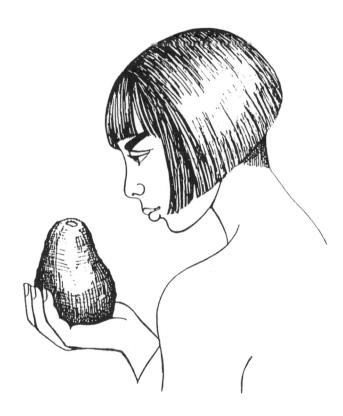

Napoleon and Josephine Salad

*Grilled new potatoes and creamy avocado
are delightful together in this simple salad.*

Yield: 6 servings
Time: 15 minutes to prepare
10–15 minutes to grill
2 hours to chill

*2 1/4 pounds new potatoes
1 tablespoon olive oil
2 tablespoons lemon juice
1 tablespoon white or yellow miso
1/4 teaspoon sea salt
1/3 cup chopped scallions
1/3 cup fresh dill weed, minced
2 small or 1 medium avocado, diced
(Add the avocado no more than 1–2 hours
before serving.)*

1. Scrub the potatoes—do not peel—and cut out any bad spots. Cut the potatoes into bite-sized pieces. Steam or pressure cook until the pieces are just tender.

2. Place the lightly cooked potatoes in a mixing bowl. Add 1 tablespoon of oil and mix well to coat with the oil. Place a rack with small holes over the bottom rack of your grill and put the potatoes on the rack. Cook over medium heat, turning often, until the potatoes are brown all over (about 5 minutes). Place the grilled potatoes in a mixing bowl and refrigerate while you prepare the remaining ingredients.

3. In a small bowl, combine the lemon juice, miso, and salt. Mix well. Pour this mixture over the potatoes and mix gently.

4. When the potatoes are cool, add the remaining ingredients. Mix gently.

Serving Suggestion

Serve over a bed of lettuce or watercress.

Swashbuckler Salad

Full of both flavor and color,
this salad will brighten up any meal.

Yield: 12 servings

Time: About 15 minutes to prepare

10–15 minutes to cook

2 red bell peppers
2 green bell peppers
2 yellow bell peppers
2 tablespoons olive oil
2 cloves garlic, pressed
1/2 teaspoon sea salt
1/4 cup finely chopped parsley

1. Wash the peppers and place them on the bottom rack of the grill over low heat. Cook them about 10–15 minutes, turning often until they begin to get soft and blistered all over.

2. Place the roasted peppers in a paper bag or a bowl with a dish towel over the top and let them cool for about 15 minutes. Remove the peppers, cut them in half lengthwise, and remove the seeds and stem. Using your hands, peel the skin off the peppers.

3. Slice the peppers into strips and place them in a bowl. Add the oil, garlic, salt, and parsley. Mix well.

4. Eat immediately or chill (will keep for 1 week).

Calliope

*Mother of the Muses, Calliope must have inspired
this vegetable medley.*

Yield: 6 servings
Time: About 10 minutes to prepare
About 10 minutes to cook
2 hours to chill

Vegetables

1 tablespoon olive oil

1 tablespoon balsamic vinegar

1 tablespoon tamari

2 cups cherry tomatoes, cut in halves

*1 1/2 cups artichoke hearts,
cut into quarters (1 can)*

8–10 cloves garlic, peeled

1 cup pitted green olives

1 cup pitted black olives

1 1/2 cups chick peas, cooked and drained

Dressing

1 tablespoon olive oil

1/2 tablespoon balsamic vinegar

1 teaspoon basil

1/2 teaspoon oregano

1 tablespoon tamari, if desired

1. In a mixing bowl, combine 1 tablespoon olive oil, 1 tablespoon
    balsamic vinegar, and 1 tablespoon tamari. Mix well and add
    the cherry tomatoes. Stir to coat the tomatoes with the mix-
    ture.

2. Place a rack with small holes over the bottom rack of your

grill. Remove the cherry tomatoes from the bowl with a slotted spoon and place them on the grill. Cook for about 3 minutes, turning the tomatoes with a spatula as needed. Place the tomatoes in another bowl.

3. Place the artichoke hearts in the bowl in which you mixed the tomatoes. Stir to coat the artichokes with the remaining sauce. Place the artichoke hearts on the grill and cook for about 3 minutes, turning as needed. Place the grilled artichoke hearts in the bowl with the tomatoes.

4. Place a small sheet of heavy-duty aluminum foil on the top rack of the grill. Put the garlic on the foil and cook over low heat, turning often, until it is brown and tender (5–10 minutes). Slice the roasted garlic into slivers and add to the bowl with the artichokes and tomatoes.

5. Add the olives and chick peas to the grilled vegetable mixture. Add the dressing ingredients, except for the optional tamari, and mix well. Taste the salad and, if desired, add the extra tamari. Chill before serving.

Serving Suggestion

To serve this salad hot, you may very briefly grill the chick peas and olives before adding them to the grilled tomatoes and artichoke hearts (no oil is needed). Add the dressing and serve immediately.

❧ *BARBECUE TIDBIT* ❧

When cooking an entire meal on the grill, start with the slowest cooking foods on the top rack. When they are almost done, start grilling the faster cooking foods on the bottom rack, leaving the slower cooking foods to finish cooking on top. ❑

Aprés Midi Salad

*We tried this recipe just for fun, not thinking that it would
really work, and were surprised when it was
a dinner-party favorite.*

Yield: 4 servings
Time: 10 minutes to prepare
10 minutes to cook

*2 1/2 cups whole-grain macaroni
(Choose macaroni that is a little larger than the
usual elbows. Quinoa pasta is especially good.)
20 cherry tomatoes, cut into halves
3 tablespoons olive oil
1/2 cup chopped scallions
1/2 cup finely chopped parsley
3 tablespoons balsamic vinegar
3 tablespoons tamari*

1. Cook the macaroni in boiling water according to the directions on the package. Drain and rinse.

2. Place the macaroni in a large bowl. Add the cherry tomatoes and the oil. Mix well. Place a rack with small holes on the bottom rack of your grill. Transfer the macaroni mixture to the rack and cook over medium-low heat, stirring often with a spatula, for 3–5 minutes or until the tomatoes are hot.

3. Gently return the mixture to the bowl. Add the remaining ingredients and serve immediately.

Pasta Salad Gourmand

*Vicki once made this salad so she'd have something
to eat at a BBQ where only meat was being served,
but it didn't work because everyone wanted
to eat the salad!*

Yield: 6 servings
Time: About 10 minutes to prepare
25–30 minutes to cook
2 hours to chill

Dressing

2 tablespoons olive oil or walnut oil
1 1/2 tablespoons balsamic vinegar
2 1/2 tablespoons tamari
4 scallions, chopped
3 cloves garlic, pressed

Salad

1 cup walnuts
1 pound asparagus
1 teaspoon olive oil
1 red bell pepper, diced
1 yellow bell pepper, diced
1 teaspoon olive oil
8 ounces whole-grain pasta ribbons
1/4 cup fresh basil, minced

1. In a small bowl, combine all the ingredients for the dressing. Set aside.

2. Coarsely chop the walnuts and place them in an ovenproof pan. Bake at 350°F for about 10 minutes, or until the walnuts are lightly roasted. (A toaster oven's small size makes it just right for this job.) Stir once or twice as they cook to make sure that they brown evenly. Set aside.

3. Wash the asparagus and snap off the tough bottom ends. Cut the spears into 1-inch pieces and place them in a medium-sized bowl. Add 1 teaspoon of oil and stir to coat the asparagus with the oil. Place a rack with small holes on the bottom rack of your grill. Place the asparagus on the rack and cook over low heat, stirring often, until the asparagus is just tender (3–5 minutes).

4. Place the asparagus in a large mixing bowl and refrigerate.

5. Place the red and yellow peppers in a medium-sized mixing bowl and add 1 teaspoon of oil. Mix well to coat the peppers with the oil. Grill over low heat, stirring often, until just tender (about 5–8 minutes). Place the grilled peppers in the bowl with the asparagus. Chill.

6. Cook the pasta ribbons in a large pot of boiling water according to the directions on the box. Drain and rinse in cold water. Add the pasta to the roasted vegetables in the mixing bowl. Add the dressing and mix gently.

7. When the salad is cool, add the fresh basil and the walnuts. Mix gently before serving.

Cybele's Salad

*Whole-grain pasta, cashews, and a bevy of vegetables
are the gifts of Cybele, the ancient Asian goddess
of the earth.*

Yield: 4–6 servings

Time: About 5 minutes to prepare

25 minutes to cook

About 2 hours to chill

Salad

1 cup raw unsalted cashews
2 medium zucchini, sliced
1 large red pepper, cut into squares
2 cups halved, medium-sized mushrooms
1 tablespoon olive oil
1 tablespoon tamari
8 ounces whole-grain pasta spirals
1/2 cup finely chopped parsley
1/2 cup finely chopped scallions

Dressing

2 tablespoons olive oil
2 tablespoons balsamic vinegar
1 teaspoon herbes de Provence
3 cloves garlic, pressed

1. Place the cashews in a baking dish and bake at 350°F for 10–15
    minutes, or until they give off a fragrant odor and are lightly
    roasted. (A toaster oven's small size makes it just right for this
    job.) Stir the cashews occasionally while they bake to make
    sure that they brown evenly. Set aside.

2. While the nuts are roasting, combine the zucchini, red pepper,
    and mushrooms in a large bowl. Add 1 tablespoon olive oil

and 1 tablespoon tamari. Mix well. Place a rack with small holes over the bottom rack of your grill. Transfer the vegetables to the rack and cook over low heat, stirring often, until they are tender but still crisp (10 minutes or less). Put a large kettle of water on to boil while the vegetables are cooking.

3. Place the roasted vegetables in a salad bowl and chill.

4. Cook the pasta in boiling water according to the directions on the package. Drain the pasta and rinse briefly under cool water.

5. Add the cooked pasta to the vegetables. Add the parsley and scallions.

6. In a small bowl, combine the ingredients for the dressing. Pour this dressing over the vegetables and pasta. Mix well and refrigerate about 2 hours.

7. Add the cashews and mix again just before serving.

Seduction Salad

*The black strands of arame, a sea vegetable,
give this rice and asparagus salad an exotic appearance.*

Yield: 6 servings
Time: 15–20 minutes to soak arame
About 5 minutes to prepare
About 15 minutes to cook
2–3 hours to chill

*1/3 cup arame
2 tablespoons tamari
1 teaspoon toasted sesame oil
1 tablespoon water
1 pound asparagus
2 teaspoons oil, divided
1 green bell pepper, diced
3 scallions, chopped
4 cups cooked and still warm
brown basmati rice
2 tablespoons rice vinegar
1 teaspoon toasted sesame oil*

1. Place the arame in a medium-sized bowl. Cover with water and let soak for 15–20 minutes. Drain the arame through a wire strainer and rinse it. Place the arame in a saucepan with the tamari, 1 teaspoon toasted sesame oil, and the water. Bring the liquid to a boil. Reduce the heat and simmer, stirring often, for about 10 minutes or until the liquid has evaporated. Transfer to a large bowl and set aside.

2. Wash the asparagus and snap off the tough bottom ends. Place the asparagus spears in a shallow dish.

3. Drizzle 1 teaspoon of oil over the asparagus and roll the

spears around in the dish to coat them with the oil. Drizzle the remaining teaspoon of oil over the pepper, and mix to coat. Place a rack with small holes on the bottom rack of the grill. Place the asparagus on one half of the rack and the pepper on the other half. Cook over low heat until the vegetables are grilled and tender (about 3–4 minutes for the asparagus and about 5 minutes for the pepper). Turn the vegetables often as they cook.

4. Chop the grilled asparagus into 1-inch pieces and transfer them to the bowl with the arame. Add the bell pepper and all the remaining ingredients. Mix well. Refrigerate until well chilled (2–3 hours). Mix and serve.

Serving Suggestion

This salad is a nice dish to accompany kebobs or grilled tofu, seitan, or tempeh dishes.

Sauces and Relishes

Sauces and relishes can enhance your grilled recipes and provide an opportunity to be creative. An ordinary meal can become special when served with the right sauce or assortment of relishes. We suggest ways to serve our sauces, but we are sure that you can discover others.

For an easy backyard party, serve grilled tofu wieners with three types of homemade relishes, and see how quickly they go. For a quick meal that is nice enough to serve to guests, grill an assortment of your favorite vegetables, serve them over whole-grain pasta or grilled polenta (page 101), and top them with our Madonna Sauce (page 81). Accompany with Romeo Rolls (page 100) and a dessert of grilled fruit (pages 183–210). Grilled tofu, which is rather bland by itself, is delicious with one of our BBQ sauces or with Teriyaki Sauce (page 87). Plain grilled vegetables with Dionysian Dill Sauce (page 77) or Balm of Gilead (page 78) are scrumptious. Add some brown rice or pasta, and you have a nutritious meal.

Those accustomed to buying bottled BBQ or tomato sauce are in for a pleasant surprise when they try these sauces. Not only are they easy to make (some of them don't take more than five minutes), but they taste so much better than commercial brands. There is also no reason to feel guilty serving any of these sauces or relishes; none of them contains cholesterol, most of them are low in fat, and some do not contain any fat. So have fun; mix and match these sauces with your favorite recipes and watch the food disappear.

Sarong Sauce

Use to marinate tofu or tempeh then thicken into a sauce.
This sauce is very good made with canned pineapple
juice, but it's exquisite made from freshly extracted juice.

Yield: About 1 1/2 cups

Time: 5 minutes to prepare

1 1/2 cups unsweetened pineapple juice
2 tablespoons tamari
1 tablespoon umeboshi vinegar
2 cloves garlic, pressed
1/2 teaspoon cumin
1/2 teaspoon coriander
pinch of cayenne, to taste
1 tablespoon + 1 teaspoon arrowroot

1. Mix together all the above ingredients, except the arrowroot.

2. Add the arrowroot, mixing well to dissolve. Place the mixture in a saucepan and bring it to a boil while stirring constantly. If the sauce becomes too thick, just add a little water to thin it to the desired consistency.

Serving Suggestion

Serve over Tropical Kebobs (page 177) or over grilled tofu. This sauce can also be used over mixed vegetable or rice dishes.

Variation

Sarong Marinade

Prepare Sarong Sauce without adding arrowroot. To marinate tempeh, first steam it for 10 minutes. Place tempeh or tofu in the liquid. Let marinate for about 1 hour. Remove the tofu or the tempeh from the liquid with a slotted spoon. If you are going to grill tofu, brush it with 1–2 tablespoons of oil and grill over medium-low heat until it is brown on both sides.

Magnificent Seven Sauce

With a barbecue sauce this good,
no one will miss the meat!

Yield: About 1 1/2 cups

Time: 5–10 minutes to prepare

1 small can (5 1/2 ounces) tomato paste
1/2 cup molasses
1 teaspoon liquid smoke
1/2 teaspoon cinnamon
1/2 teaspoon allspice
2 cloves garlic, pressed
2 tablespoons tamari
1 tablespoon balsamic vinegar
pinch of cayenne

1. In a medium-sized bowl, mix together the tomato paste and the molasses.

2. Add the remaining ingredients and mix well.

Serving Suggestion

This sauce is good with grilled tofu, tempeh, seitan, veggie burgers, or kebobs. Leftover sauce will keep very well in a covered container in the refrigerator.

Island Barbecue Sauce

Add an exotic flair to your grilled menu.

Yield: About 1 1/4 cups

Time: 5–10 minutes to prepare

1 small can (5 1/2 ounces) tomato paste
1/4 cup molasses
1/4 cup pineapple juice
1 clove garlic, pressed
1 tablespoon rice vinegar
2 tablespoons tamari
1/2 teaspoon Chinese five spice

1. In a medium-sized bowl, mix together the tomato paste and molasses.

2. Add the remaining ingredients and mix well.

Serving Suggestion

This sauce is great with grilled tofu, tempeh, or seitan. It is also good with veggie burgers.

❧ *BARBECUE TIDBIT* ❧

One teaspoon (more or less to taste) of liquid smoke can be added to the cooking oil or the marinade of most recipes for added smoke flavor. ❑

Caprice Cashew Sauce

Dijon-style mustard, named for a town in the Burgundy region of France, spices up this velvety sauce.

Yield: About 2 1/2 cups
Time: About 5 minutes to prepare
About 5 minutes to cook

2/3 cup raw unsalted cashews
1 1/4 cups water
1 tablespoon Dijon-style mustard
2 tablespoons nutritional yeast
1/2 teaspoon turmeric
pinch of cayenne, to taste
2 tablespoons yellow or white miso

1. Place all the above ingredients, except the miso, in a blender. Blend until very smooth and creamy. (Make sure to blend the ingredients long enough or the cashews will be gritty.)

2. Place the mixture in a saucepan. While stirring constantly, bring the mixture to a boil. Reduce the heat and simmer until the sauce has thickened.

3. Remove the sauce from the heat and add the miso. Mix well to dissolve the miso. If the sauce becomes too thick, add a little water.

Serving Suggestion

This sauce is delicious over grilled vegetables, such as sweet potatoes, asparagus, or zucchini. It is also good over Pocahontas's Polenta (page 101).

Dionysian Dill Sauce

This easy and pretty sauce has a wonderful texture.

Yield: About 1 1/2 cups

Time: About 5 minutes to prepare

1 package (10.5 ounces) soft silken tofu
2 tablespoons white or yellow miso
1/4 cup fresh dill
2 scallions, chopped
pinch of cayenne

1. Place all the above ingredients in a blender.
2. Blend until smooth and creamy. Use a rubber spatula to scrape the sides of the blender if necessary to make sure that the mixture gets well blended.

Serving Suggestion

This sauce is delicious over grilled vegetables, such as artichokes, asparagus, potatoes, endives, or over steamed vegetables, such as broccoli or cauliflower.

Variations

Zesty Dionysian Dill Sauce

Add 1 teaspoon Dijon-style mustard and increase the dill up to 1/3 cup maximum. You may also add an extra scallion.

Dionysian Dill Sauce With Firm Tofu

Substitute an equal amount of firm tofu for the soft silken tofu. Add 1–2 tablespoons of soy milk to the ingredients in the blender for firm tofu. Add 3–4 tablespoons of soy milk if you substitute extra-firm tofu.

Balm of Gilead

*Delicious over raw or grilled vegetables,
creamy Balm of Gilead gets its distinctive taste
from balsamic vinegar, a sweet wine vinegar.*

Yield: About 1 cup

Time: About 10 minutes to prepare

*1/2 cup mashed firm silken tofu
1/2 cup raw unsalted cashews
2 tablespoons tamari
2 tablespoons balsamic vinegar
1/2 teaspoon tarragon
1 clove garlic, pressed*

1. Place the cashews in a blender and blend to a powder. (Do not try to do this in a food processor because the cashews will not be ground finely enough.)

2. Place the remaining ingredients in a food processor. Add the cashew powder and blend until the sauce is smooth and creamy. (You can do this in a blender, but if it is not a powerful blender, you will probably have to blend in two batches. Mix all the ingredients together and divide the mix in half before blending.)

Serving Suggestion

This sauce is wonderful over grilled sweet potatoes, potatoes, zucchini, or artichokes. It is also good as a dip for raw vegetables or as a dressing for green salad.

Siam Sauce

Spicy peanut sauce is fit for Anna's King.
Even people who don't like peanut butter usually love it!

Yield: About 2 1/4 cups

Time: 5 minutes to prepare

5 minutes to cook

3/4 cup natural peanut butter
(smooth or crunchy)
2–3 tablespoons tamari, to taste
2 cloves garlic, pressed
1 1/2 tablespoons lemon juice
1 1/4 cups water
pinch of cayenne to taste

1. Place the peanut butter in a saucepan. Add the tamari, garlic, and lemon juice. Mix well. Gradually stir in the water to make a creamy consistency.

2. Place the saucepan over medium heat and bring the sauce to a boil while stirring constantly. Cook until thickened. Add the cayenne. (If the sauce becomes too thick, add enough water to achieve the desired consistency.)

Serving Suggestion

Serve this sauce over Indonesian Delight (page 142).

Pesto de Venus

The avocado in this sauce is highly nutritious.
In comparison to other fruits, avocados have low water
content and contain protein, mineral salts,
and many vitamins.

Yield: About 1 1/2 cups

Time: About 10 minutes to prepare

1 cup mashed ripe avocado
1 1/2 cups basil leaves
1/2 teaspoon sea salt
2 teaspoons lemon juice

1. Place all of the above ingredients in a blender or food processor.

2. Blend until smooth and creamy. Scrape the sides of the blender or food processor with a rubber spatula as needed to make sure the mixture is well blended.

3. Serve immediately as this sauce will darken if it is not used soon after it is made.

Serving Suggestion

Pesto de Venus is good over Intermezzo (page 120) or with a pasta salad or green salad.

Madonna Sauce

*It's almost as easy as opening a can of tomato sauce,
but fresh is so much better.*

Yield: About 2 1/2 cups

Time: About 5 minutes to prepare

About 20 minutes to cook

*1 tablespoon olive oil
2 cloves garlic, minced
3 bay leaves
1 teaspoon oregano
1 teaspoon basil
1/3 cup finely chopped onion
3 medium tomatoes, coarsely chopped
2 tablespoons tomato paste
1/4 teaspoon sea salt*

1. Heat the oil in a skillet. Add the garlic, bay leaves, oregano, basil, and onion. Sauté over medium heat until the onion is tender.

2. While the onion is cooking, place the chopped tomatoes in a blender or food processor and blend them into a purée. This will probably have to be done in two batches.

3. Add the tomato purée to the sautéed onion mixture. Add the tomato paste and the salt. Let the sauce simmer, uncovered, over low heat for 10–15 minutes.

Serving Suggestion

This sauce is delicious with Pocahontas's Polenta (page 101) or Garden Grill (page 118). It is also good with rice, pasta, or veggie burgers, or grilled tofu or tempeh.

Victoria's Secret Sauce

*The secret of turning an ordinary jar of tomato sauce
into something etraordinary is the addition
of roasted vegetables!*

Yield: 4 servings
Time: About 10 minutes to prepare
25–30 minutes to grill
5 minutes to cook

2 cups tomato sauce, canned or homemade
2 cups coarsely chopped onions
1 teaspoon olive oil
1 red bell pepper, diced
1 green bell pepper, diced
1 teaspoon olive oil
8 cloves garlic
*12 ounces mushrooms, cut into halves
or quarters (depending on size)*
1 teaspoon oregano
4 bay leaves
pinch of cayenne
1 tablespoon tamari

1. Place the tomato sauce in a large saucepan. Set aside.

2. In a mixing bowl, combine the onions and 1 teaspoon of oil. Mix well to coat the onions with the oil. Place a rack with small holes over the bottom rack of your grill. Place the onions on the rack and cook over low heat, stirring often, until they are done (about 5–8 minutes). Transfer the onions to the large pan with the tomato sauce. Set aside.

3. In a mixing bowl, combine the peppers and 1 teaspoon of oil.

Mix well to coat the peppers with the oil. Place the peppers on the grill and cook over low heat, stirring often, until they are done (5–8 minutes). Transfer the peppers to the pan with the tomato sauce. Set aside.

4. Place the garlic on the top rack of the grill in a small metal pan or on a sheet of foil. Cook, turning often, until it is brown and tender (5–8 minutes). Chop the garlic and add it to the sauce.

5. Place the mushrooms on the grill without oil and cook, stirring often, until they are done (about 5 minutes). Add the mushrooms to the sauce.

6. Add the oregano, bay leaves, cayenne, and tamari to the sauce. Mix well and bring to a simmer. Cook over low heat for about 5 minutes. Remove the bay leaves before serving.

Serving Suggestion

Serve over whole-grain spaghetti and garnish with fresh basil, finely chopped.

Reveler's Relish

*For a large American-style cookout, Vicki served healthy
versions of traditional foods, including potato salad and
coleslaw, but the hit of the party was the tofu wieners
cooked on the grill and served with this relish.*

Yield: About 4 cups*

Time: About 20 minutes

---

*1 red bell pepper
1 green bell pepper
1 yellow bell pepper
1 cucumber (peel if waxed)
1/2 cup finely chopped red onion
1/2 cup cider vinegar
1/4 cup honey
1/2 teaspoon sea salt
1/2 teaspoon dry mustard powder
1/2 teaspoon ground celery seeds
1/2 teaspoon cinnamon
1/4 teaspoon allspice*

1. Remove seeds from the peppers. Finely chop the peppers and
   the cucumber.

2. Combine chopped vegetables with the remaining ingredients.

3. This relish can be eaten right away but it is better if allowed
   to sit for several hours. Store it in a covered container in the
   refrigerator.

---

* This is a rather large quantity of relish, but it keeps very well in the
refrigerator for 2–3 weeks. You may cut the recipe in half, if you want a
smaller quantity.

Melodious Maize

Deliciously different from a store-bought relish,
Melodious Maize is a colorful sweet corn relish.

Yield: About 2 1/2 cups

Time: 15–20 minutes to prepare

3 cups sweet corn, cut off the cob
1 cup water or sufficient to cover bottom of pan
1/3 cup red onion, finely chopped
1/3 cup green bell pepper, finely chopped
1/3 cup red bell pepper, finely chopped
1/4 cup apple cider vinegar
1/4 cup honey
1 teaspoon sea salt
2 teaspoons pink peppercorns
1/4 teaspoon turmeric

1. Steam the corn or cook in a pan with about 1 cup of water for 3–5 minutes or until it is tender. (To steam, place the corn in a vegetable steamer or metal colander. Place the steamer in a large pan with about 1/2 inch of water in the bottom of the pan. Cover the pan and bring the water to a boil. Reduce the heat to medium-low and steam.)

2. Place the corn in a mixing bowl. Add the remaining ingredients and mix well.

Serving Suggestion

This relish can be served immediately, but tastes better if allowed to sit for several hours. Store in a covered container in the refrigerator. Serve Melodious Maize with burgers, vegetable croquettes, or tofu wieners. It is also wonderful with Pocahontas's Polenta (page 101).

Garden of Delights Relish

Several delights from the garden make this tomato relish
more delectable than the catsup it resembles.

Yield: About 2 1/2 cups
Time: About 20 minutes to prepare
5 minutes to cook
2 hours or more to marinate

2 pounds Italian plum tomatoes
water sufficient to cover bottom of kettle
1/3 cup finely chopped red onion
1 cup finely chopped red bell pepper (1 medium)
2 tablespoons balsamic vinegar
1/4 cup honey
1/2 teaspoon sea salt
16 sun-dried tomato halves

1. Place the Italian plum tomatoes in a vegetable steamer or a large wire strainer. Place the steamer in a large kettle with about 1 inch of water in the bottom. Cover and bring the water to a boil. Reduce the heat to medium and steam for about 5 minutes. Remove the tomatoes from the pan and let them sit until they are cool enough to handle. Carefully peel the skin off the tomatoes.

2. Finely chop the steamed tomatoes and place them in a bowl. When all the tomatoes are chopped, drain off the excess juice that has accumulated in the bottom of the bowl. Reserve the juice to use in soups or sauces.

3. Add the onion, bell pepper, vinegar, honey, and salt.

4. Place the sun-dried tomato halves in a blender and grind. Add the ground dried tomatoes to the relish. Mix well and let marinate for at least 2 hours.

Serving Suggestion

This relish is delicious over veggie burgers, tofu wieners, tofu, tempeh, seitan dishes, or kebobs. Store it in a covered container in the refrigerator.

Variation

Spicy Garden of Delights Relish

Add ½ teaspoon cinnamon, ½ teaspoon celery seeds, ⅛ teaspoon cloves, ½ teaspoon paprika, and a pinch of cayenne to the relish.

Teriyaki Sauce

Try our version of an Oriental favorite.

Yield: About 1/2 cup

Time: 5 minutes to prepare

1 teaspoon toasted sesame oil
1/4 cup tamari
2 tablespoons mixed-fruit-concentrate
sweetener
2 cloves garlic, pressed
1 tablespoon rice vinegar
1 tablespoon finely grated fresh ginger
pinch of cayenne

1. In a small bowl, mix together all the ingredients.

Serving Suggestion

Use this sauce to marinate tofu, tempeh, or seitan before grilling, or serve it on the side to spice up grilled tofu, tempeh, or seitan dishes. It is also good with grilled vegetables or grain dishes.

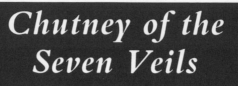

Chutney of the Seven Veils

*Chutney is a highly spiced relish consisting of fruits,
spices, vinegar, and sweetener.
Chutney of the Seven Veils is sweet and mild.*

Yield: About 2 cups

Time: 10 minutes to prepare

About 20 minutes to cook

---

*3 1/2 cups peeled and chopped peaches
(3 medium)*

1 tablespoon rice vinegar

2 tablespoons honey

1/4 teaspoon turmeric

1/2 teaspoon coriander

1 teaspoon finely grated fresh ginger

1. Combine all the above ingredients in a saucepan. Bring the mixture to a boil.

2. Reduce the heat and simmer, uncovered, for about 20 minutes, stirring occasionally.

Serving Suggestion

This chutney is good with Kamasutra Curry (page 150).

Variation

Spicy Chutney of the Seven Veils

Add a little more vinegar, 2 teaspoons more fresh ginger, and a pinch of cayenne.

Pizzas, Breads, and Sandwiches

Focaccia—a flat, yeasted herb-bread—and pizza are both surprisingly fast and easy to cook on the grill. Grilling makes the bottom of the crust crispy brown, and the top stays nice and soft. The results are more like pizza made in a good restaurant than in a home oven.

The most important thing to remember when cooking pizza or focaccia is to cook it on the top rack of the grill and not to over-cook it. Ten minutes is usually the maximum, and sometimes that is just a bit too long. In fact, we have had pizzas ready in six minutes. It all depends on the temperature of the grill when you start. The flame should be turned to low, but the heat indicator should be at medium. If the indicator reads hotter than medium, open the lid of the grill for a couple of minutes until the temperature cools down a little. If the grill gets too hot while you are cooking pizza, you can turn the gas all the way off after about five minutes, and let the pizza cook without flames for three to five minutes more.

If your first pizza does not succeed, do not be discouraged. Try again; we are sure that you will get the hang of it. Once you master the art of baking pizza on the grill, you may never want to bake it in an oven again.

Of course, you never did need your oven to prepare sandwiches. But now, using your grill and your imagination, sandwiches will become a feast in themselves. This chapter includes a few recipes for sandwiches using grilled foods, but the possibilities are endless. Listed below are a few other sandwich suggestions, but please feel free to experiment: make substitutions or create your own sandwiches. Just remember to use a variety of whole-grain breads, burger buns, hot dog rolls, pita bread, chapaties, sprouted breads, whole-wheat French bread, sourdough breads, etc. Having a good fresh bread is the first step in creating a great sandwich.

- Grilled eggplant, zucchini, and onions with melted soy cheese on whole-grain French or Italian bread.
- Grilled tofu or tempeh, brushed generously with one of our BBQ sauces, served on a whole-wheat bun, and topped with lettuce or sprouts.
- Chisum Chili (page 51) on an open-faced whole-wheat bun. Top with chopped scallions.
- Tempeh—cut into sandwich-sized pieces, steamed for about 10 minutes, brushed with tamari and then lightly with oil, and grilled—served on rye bread with mashed avocado and sauerkraut.
- Steamed and grilled tempeh (see above) served with roasted red peppers, mustard, and lettuce on sliced whole-wheat bread.
- The Joy of Tofu (page 143) with slices of ripe tomato, mustard, onion, and lettuce.

Focaccia

Called "fougasse" in French, this bread is served in the south of France and in Italy.

Yield: 1 bread (6 servings)
Time: 25 minutes to prepare
About 2 hours to rise
About 8 minutes to grill

Bread

1 cup lukewarm water

2 tablespoons oil

1 teaspoon honey

1 tablespoon dry active yeast

1/4 teaspoon sea salt

1 tablespoon Vital Wheat Gluten

2 1/4 cups whole-wheat bread flour (approximately)

Topping

3 tablespoons olive oil

1 teaspoon oregano

1 teaspoon finely chopped fresh rosemary (1/2 teaspoon dry)

2 tablespoons finely chopped fresh basil (1 teaspoon dry)

4 cloves garlic, pressed

1/4 teaspoon sea salt

1/2 tablespoon onion powder

1. In a large bowl, combine the water, oil, honey, and yeast. Let the mixture sit for about 10 minutes to dissolve the yeast.

2. Add the salt, the Vital Wheat Gluten, and about 1 cup of the bread flour. Beat the dough 100 strokes with a wooden spoon.

3. Gradually stir in enough of the remaining flour so that the dough pulls away from the sides of the bowl. Place the dough on a floured surface and knead for about 10 minutes, kneading in enough flour to make the dough smooth and elastic but not too sticky. (This dough can be a little stickier than an ordinary bread dough.)

4. Place the dough in a lightly oiled bowl. Turn the dough over to oil the top. Place the bowl in a warm place and let the dough rise until it is double in bulk (about 1 hour).

5. To shape the bread, generously oil a 10-inch x 16-inch cookie sheet. With your hands, press the dough out onto the sheet to cover it with an even thickness. Cover the dough with a damp cloth and let it rise for about 20 minutes.

6. In a small bowl, combine all the topping ingredients. Spread this mixture over the dough. Cover the dough with a piece of aluminum foil. Make sure that the foil bubbles up and is not flat against the dough.

7. Place the cookie sheet on the top rack of your grill. Cook over low heat for about 8 minutes. To test for doneness, peel back the foil and pinch off a little of the top crust of the bread. When it is done, the bread will not be gooey.

Serving Suggestion

Serve hot, sliced into squares. Focaccia is very good with a soup or stew. It is also good with Intermezzo (page 120) and Pesto de Venus (page 80).

To reheat this bread, place it under the broiler or in a toaster oven for 2–3 minutes.

Pizza Provençal

Here's a light and easy fresh-tomato pizza

Yield: 6 servings
Time: 25 minutes to prepare
About 1 1/2 hours to rise
About 8 minutes to grill

Crust
1 cup lukewarm water
2 tablespoons oil
1 teaspoon honey
1 tablespoon dry active yeast
1/4 teaspoon sea salt
1 tablespoon Vital Wheat Gluten
2 1/4 cups whole-wheat bread flour
(approximately)

Topping
8 cloves garlic, pressed
1 tablespoon herbes de Provence
2 tablespoons olive oil
1/2 teaspoon sea salt
3 large tomatoes, sliced
1/4 cup tofu parmesan (optional)

1. In a large bowl, combine the water, oil, honey, and yeast. Let the mix sit for about 10 minutes to dissolve the yeast.

2. Add the salt, the Vital Wheat Gluten, and about 1 cup of the bread flour. Beat the dough 100 strokes with a wooden spoon.

3. Gradually stir in enough of the remaining flour so that the dough pulls away from the sides of the bowl. Place the dough

on a floured surface and knead for bout 10 minutes, kneading in enough flour to make the dough smooth and elastic but not too sticky. (This dough can be a little stickier than an ordinary bread dough.)

4. Place the dough in a lightly oiled bowl. Turn the dough over to oil the top. Place the bowl in a warm place and let the dough rise until it is double in bulk (about 1 hour).

5. Generously oil a 10-inch x 16-inch cookie sheet. With your hands, press the dough out onto the sheet so that it covers the sheet with an even thickness. Lightly cover the dough with a damp cloth and let it sit while you prepare the topping.

6. In a small bowl, combine the garlic, herbs, olive oil, and salt. Brush this mixture over the pizza.

7. Cover the pizza with the tomato slices (do not use the end slices). Sprinkle with the tofu parmesan, if desired.

8. Cover the dough with a sheet of aluminum foil. Place the foil so that it bubbles up a little and is not flat against the pizza.

9. Place the cookie sheet on the top rack of the grill. Cook over low heat for about 8 minutes. To test for doneness, peel back the foil and pinch off a little from the center of the top of the crust. When it is done, the crust will not be gooey.

Athena's Pizza

*As tempting as the goddess herself, this pizza bears
Athena's name because of her association with the olive.
According to one myth, Athena brought forth an olive tree
in an attempt to prove her superiority over Poseidon.
Since a crown of olive branches was the traditional gift
to the victor, Athena was automatically the winner.
The combination of olives, tempeh, and onion in this
pizza will be a winner with you!*

Yield: 4–6 servings
Time: About 20 minutes to prepare
About 1 1/2 hours to rise
About 8 minutes to grill

crust recipe from Pizza Provençal (page 93)

*1/2 pound tempeh (one package),
thawed if frozen and cut into tiny cubes*

water sufficient to steam tempeh

2 cups chopped onions

4 cloves garlic, minced

1–2 teaspoons olive oil

1 cup sliced black olives

1/2 teaspoon thyme

1 teaspoon basil

1/2 teaspoon oregano

2 tablespoons tamari

1/4 cup water

2 tablespoons nutritional yeast

1 tablespoon olive oil

1. Prepare the pizza crust up to step 4 and let it rise in a warm place while you make the filling.

2. Place the tempeh in a vegetable steamer and steam over boiling water for about 10 minutes.

3. While the tempeh is steaming, sauté the onions and garlic in 1–2 teaspoons olive oil until they are tender.

4. In a large bowl, combine the steamed tempeh, sautéed onions and garlic, sliced olives, herbs, tamari, water, and yeast. Mix well and slightly mash the tempeh with a fork.

5. Using your hands, press the dough out onto a 10-inch x 16-inch cookie sheet to cover it with an even thickness. Top it with the tempeh mixture. Drizzle with 1 tablespoon of olive oil.

6. Cover the dough with a sheet of aluminum foil. Place the foil over the cookie sheet so that it bubbles up a little and is not flat against the pizza.

7. Place the cookie sheet on the top rack of the grill. Cook over low heat for about 8 minutes. To test for doneness, peel back the foil and pinch off a little from the center of the top of the crust. When it is done, the crust will not be gooey.

Gable's Grill

Tired of the same old sandwiches for lunch?
Try this grilled mushroom sandwich for something
deliciously different. You'll give a damn, for sure.

Yield: 4 servings
Time: 15 minutes to prepare
12–13 minutes to grill

1 tablespoon oil
2 tablespoons tamari
4 thin slices Spanish onion
2 cups of sliced, medium-sized mushrooms
8 slices whole-grain bread
mustard or mayonnaise, to taste
4 slices tomato
1 cup grated cheddar-style soy cheese

1. In a large bowl, mix together the oil and the tamari. Lightly brush both sides of each onion slice with this mixture.

2. Add the mushrooms to the bowl and mix well to coat with the remaining oil/tamari mixture. Place a rack with small holes on the bottom rack of your grill. Place the onion slices along the sides of the rack. Let the onions cook for 2–3 minutes over low heat and then place the mushrooms next to the onions. Turn the onions when they are browned on the bottom and stir the mushrooms occasionally. Continue to cook until the onions and the mushrooms are grilled (about 10 minutes in all).

3. Spread each slice of bread with mayonnaise or mustard to taste. Place 1/4 of the grilled mushrooms, 1 slice of tomato, 1 slice of onion, and 1/4 of the soy cheese on each of 4 slices of bread.

4. Cover the ingredients with the remaining bread to make sandwiches. Place the sandwiches on the grill and cook for about 2–3 minutes on each side just to toast the bread and melt the cheese.

5. Serve immediately with a green salad.

Brave Combo Sandwich

A musical group called Brave Combo
plays a hilarious and dynamic mixture of Latin, Jewish,
American rock, and polka music. We named this funny
but delicious sandwich after this group.

Yield: 6 servings

Time: About 10 minutes to prepare

10 minutes to grill

1 1/2 cups mashed avocado
1 tablespoon balsamic vinegar
2 tablespoons Braggs Liquid Aminos (or tamari)
1/2 cup finely chopped red onion
12 tofu wieners
6 whole-grain pita breads
Dijon-style mustard, to taste
1 1/2 cups sauerkraut, drained

1. In a medium-sized bowl, combine the mashed avocado, vinegar, Braggs Liquid Aminos, and onion. Set aside.

2. Cook the wieners on the grill, over medium heat, until they are brown and crispy. Turn them often as they cook. (If desired, boil the wieners for 2–3 minutes before grilling them. Dominique says that this makes them more tender.)

3. Heat the pita bread. (We make two stacks of 3 breads on the rack of a toaster oven and cook them over high heat for 2–3 minutes. About half way through the cooking, we put the middle pita on the top, so it gets as warm as the others. The bread does not dry out this way.)

4. To assemble the sandwiches, cut the warm pitas in half and place one wiener in each half. Spread with mustard and top with the avocado mixture and sauerkraut.

Fonzie's Sandwich

It's thumbs up for this sandwich! It reminds us of the hot chicken sandwiches that were served, open-faced, with mashed potatoes and gravy in the 50s.

Yield: 4 servings
Time: About 10 minutes to prepare
10 minutes to grill

Tofu

1 pound firm tofu
1 tablespoon tamari
1/2 teaspoon liquid smoke
1–2 cloves garlic, pressed
1 tablespoon oil

Gravy

1 tablespoon oil
3 tablespoons whole-wheat pastry flour
1 1/2 cups soy milk
1/2 tablespoon Dijon-style mustard
1/2 teaspoon sea salt
pinch of cayenne

Bread

4 thick slices whole-grain bread, toasted
1–2 tablespoons minced parsley

1. Cut the tofu into 4 slabs, sized so each slab will cover 1 slice of bread.

2. In a small bowl, combine the tamari, liquid smoke, garlic, and oil. Brush this mixture over the tofu slices. Place the tofu slices on the bottom rack of the grill and cook over low heat until they are brown on the bottom. Turn them over and cook the other side (about 5 minutes each side).

3. While the tofu is cooking, make the gravy: Heat 1 tablespoon of oil in a saucepan. Add flour and mix well. While stirring constantly over medium-high heat with a wire whisk, slowly add the soy milk. Cook until thickened. Add the mustard, salt, and cayenne.

4. Place each slice of grilled tofu on a slice of whole-grain toast. Top with gravy and sprinkle with a little parsley. Serve immediately.

Romeo Rolls

*Two things always make me think "Italian"—
garlic and lovers.*

Yield: 6 servings

Time: About 2 minutes to prepare

2–3 minutes to grill

*1/4 cup olive oil
4 cloves garlic, pressed
1/4 teaspoon sea salt
6 Whole-Wheat Burger Buns (page 181)
or any whole-wheat rolls*

1. In a small bowl, combine the oil, garlic, and salt. Mix well.

2. Cut the rolls in half, if they are not pre-cut. Brush them with the garlic mixture.

3. Place the rolls on the bottom rack of the grill, cut side down, over medium heat for 2–3 minutes, or until toasted.

Serving Suggestion

Serve immediately, plain or as a base for burgers or other sandwiches.

Pocahontas's Polenta

Cornmeal is a mainstay in many ethnic diets.
Although Native Americans may have been the first
to use it, in Romania it's served with sour cream
and known as "Mama Liga."

Yield: 3–6 servings
Time: 20 minutes to prepare
3–4 hours to chill
About 10 minutes to grill

1 cup cornmeal
3 cups water
1/4 teaspoon sea salt
1 tablespoon oil

1. In a heavy, medium-sized pan, combine the cornmeal, water, and salt.

2. Bring the mixture to a boil, while stirring constantly. When the mixture boils, cover the pan and reduce the heat to low. Cook over low heat, stirring often, for 15–20 minutes. The polenta should be very thick.

3. Spread the hot polenta into a lightly oiled 8-inch x 8-inch cake pan. Refrigerate the polenta for 3–4 hours.

4. Cut the cold polenta into about 6 equal rectangles. Brush the polenta with oil. Place a rack with small holes on the bottom rack of your grill. Place the oiled polenta on the rack and cook over low heat until it is brown on the bottom (about 5 minutes). If you try to turn the polenta and it is not yet brown on the bottom, let it cook a little longer. (This polenta holds together very well, but it must be crispy and well-cooked on the bottom before you turn it or it may stick or fall apart.) Turn the polenta over and let it cook on the other side.

Serving Suggestion

Serve with Garden Grill (page 118) and Madonna Sauce (page 81). It is also good with a vegetable stew such as Babette's Feast (page 38). For a great appetizer, try grilled polenta with Melodious Maize (page 85).

Cassanova's Treat

Make this delicious Italian-tasting eggplant sandwich with leftovers.

Yield: 1 serving

Time: 5 minutes to prepare using leftovers

2 slices whole-grain bread

Dijon-style mustard, to taste

3–4 slices Bathsheba Eggplant (page 109)

4–5 slices roasted bell peppers or leftovers from Swashbuckler Salad (page 61)

3 slices Yves Veggie Pepperoni

1 leaf curly lettuce

1. Spread the bread with mustard and then pile on as much grilled eggplant and roasted peppers as will stay on the sandwich.

2. Top with 3 slices of Yves Veggie Pepperoni and a leaf of curly lettuce.

Variation

If you don't have leftover roasted peppers, substitute a slice of ripe tomato.

Side Dishes

Colorful and flavorful, grilled vegetables are the perfect accompaniment to almost any main dish. And your choices are limited only by your imagination. You can cook any vegetable on the grill—just remember to watch vegetables carefully (see page 15 for more information) so they don't burn.

In this chapter, you will find recipes for cooking an assortment of side dishes composed almost entirely of vegetables as well as suggestions for serving them. When we were experimenting with these recipes, we found that people who claim not to like certain vegetables, like them when they are grilled.

Zucchini à la Bacchus

Revelers agree—this dish has spirit!

Yield: 3–4 servings
Time: About 10 minutes to prepare
5 minutes to cook

2–3 medium zucchini
1 tablespoon olive oil
1/4 teaspoon sea salt, or to taste
1 teaspoon basil
1/2 teaspoon oregano
2 cloves garlic, pressed

1. Wash the zucchini well and cut them into thin lengthwise slices.

2. In a small bowl, combine the remaining ingredients. Brush this mixture over the tops of the zucchini slices. Place the slices on the grill, brushed side down. Brush the tops with the remaining oil/seasoning mixture. Cook for about 3 minutes or until the zucchini are lightly browned on the bottom. Turn them over and cook for about 2 minutes more, or until tender.

3. Serve immediately.

Serving Suggestion

Zucchini à la Bacchus is delicious in Apollo's Antipasto (page 34). Also use it to accompany pasta dishes.

❧ *BARBECUE TIDBIT* ❧

To keep foods from sticking, lightly brush the cooking racks with oil or spray with a nonstick coating before the grill is heated. ❏

Aphrodite's Artichokes

Even artichokes can be cooked on a grill!

Yield: 8 servings (1 artichoke per person)

Time: 5 minutes to prepare

About 40 minutes to cook

8 artichokes

1. If the artichokes are nice and fresh, cut a thin slice off of the bottom of the stem, wash the artichokes well, and, if desired, cut the sharp tips off the ends of the leaves with scissors. If the artichokes are no longer fresh, remove and discard the stems before grilling.

2. Wrap each artichoke in a piece of aluminum foil, and place on the top rack of your grill. Cook the artichokes for about 40 minutes at medium-low heat. Turn them occasionally and change their places because the artichokes in the center of the grill tend to cook faster than those on the sides.

3. When the artichokes are done, a fork or bamboo skewer can be easily inserted into the stem end, and the outer leaves will be very easy to pull off.

Serving Suggestion

Serve the artichokes with your favorite sauce or salad dressing. Try them with Dionysian Dill Sauce (page 77) or Balm of Gilead (page 78).

Eros' Endives

You'll love these endives in lemon miso sauce.

Yield: 4–6 servings
Time: 6 minutes to prepare
6 minutes to cook

Sauce

2 tablespoons lemon juice
1 tablespoon white or yellow miso
1 teaspoon tarragon
1 clove garlic, pressed

Vegetables

4–6 endives, or 1 per person
1 tablespoon olive oil, or as needed

1. In a small bowl, combine the lemon juice, miso, tarragon, and garlic. Mix well and set aside.

2. Wash the endives and remove any discolored exterior leaves. Cut the endives in half lengthwise.

3. Brush the endives with oil and place them on the grill, cut side down, over medium heat. Cook until they are slightly browned on the cut side and then turn them over to cook briefly on the other side (5–6 minutes in all).

4. Immediately transfer the endives to serving plates and drizzle a teaspoon or so of sauce over each serving. Go lightly on the sauce because it is rather strong.

5. Serve immediately.

Serving Suggestion

This dish goes particularly well with a seitan or tofu dish. You can also serve it as an appetizer.

Romancing the Squash

**Winter squash cooks quickly on the grill
and is amazingly good!**

Yield: 4–6 servings

Time: 5 minutes to prepare

10–15 minutes to cook

*1 large butternut squash
(or any kind of winter squash)
2 tablespoons olive oil
2–3 cloves garlic, pressed
1/4–1/2 teaspoon sea salt*

1. Wash the squash, cut it in half, and scrape out the seeds and membrane. Carefully cut the squash into lengthwise slices that are no more than 1-inch thick. (Winter squash is hard to cut so use a large, sharp knife and be careful not to cut yourself.)

2. In a small bowl, mix together the oil, garlic, and salt. Brush both cut sides of each slice of squash with this mixture. Place the squash slices on the bottom rack of the grill and cook over low heat until they are browned on the bottom. As the squash cooks, brush the tops with any leftover oil mixture, if desired.

3. Turn the slices over and cook on the other side until they are tender. (Total cooking time will be about 10–15 minutes.) The slices near the center of your grill will cook faster than those near the outside so during the cooking, move the slices around to keep them from burning. Move some of the slices to the top rack if necessary.

Serving Suggestion

Serve as a side dish to accompany tofu, tempeh, bean, or grain dishes.

Ceres' Grill

*The goddess who first helped man to grow crops
knew that corn would be put to excellent use.*

Yield: 6 servings
Time: 10 minutes to prepare
About 10 minutes to cook

1 teaspoon olive oil

1 red bell pepper, cut into cubes

*4 1/2 cups sweet corn, cut off the cob
(4 medium-sized ears)*

1 teaspoon olive oil

4 scallions, chopped

1 teaspoon cumin

1 teaspoon basil

1/2 teaspoon sea salt

1. In a mixing bowl, combine 1 teaspoon oil with the bell pepper. Mix well. Place a rack with small holes on the bottom rack of your grill. Place the pepper on the grill and cook over low heat until tender (about 5–8 minutes). Set the pepper aside.

2. In a mixing bowl, combine the corn with the remaining teaspoon of oil. Mix well and gently transfer the corn to the rack. Cook for about 3 minutes without stirring.

3. Stir gently, being careful not to let the corn fall through the holes of the rack (a little will fall through, but not very much if you are careful). Cook for 2–3 minutes more.

4. Transfer the corn to a serving bowl. Add the pepper, scallions, cumin, basil, and salt. Mix well and serve immediately.

Serving Suggestion

Enjoy this dish with Seven Samurai Tofu (page 146). It is also good with any bean or Mexican style dish.

Bathsheba Eggplant

This is simple, easy and, we think,
one of the best ways to cook eggplant.

Yield: 8 servings

Time: 10 minutes to prepare

About 10 minutes to cook

2 medium eggplants (1 pound each)
2 tablespoons olive oil
2 tablespoons tamari
1 tablespoon balsamic vinegar
4 cloves garlic, pressed

1. Slice the eggplants into 1/2-inch rounds. In a small bowl, combine the oil, tamari, vinegar, and garlic. Brush this mixture over the eggplant rounds.

2. Place the rounds (as many as will easily fit in one layer) on the bottom rack of the grill. Cook over low heat until they are brown on the bottom (3–4 minutes). Turn them over and cook for 3–4 minutes more, or until the other side is browned.

Serving Suggestion

Don't worry about cooking too much eggplant, because it is delicious cold in sandwiches (see Cassanova's Treat on page 102) or in Apollo's Antipasto (page 34).

Opie's Okra

*Okra always makes me think of barefoot boys
squishing Mississippi mud between their toes.
Okra is also known as "gumbo"; whatever you call it,
it's really good grilled.*

Yield: 4 servings

Time: 10 minutes to prepare

15 minutes to cook

*1 pound okra
2 tablespoons oil
1/3 cup cornmeal
1/2 teaspoon sea salt, or to taste*

1. Wash the okra and cut off the stem ends. Slice the okra into 1/2-inch rounds.

2. Place the okra in a mixing bowl and drizzle the oil over it. Mix well to coat the okra with the oil.

3. In a small bowl, mix together the cornmeal and the salt. Sprinkle the cornmeal/salt mixture over the okra and mix well to coat the okra with the cornmeal. Place a rack with small holes on the bottom rack of the grill. Transfer the okra to the rack and cook over low heat, stirring often, for 3–5 minutes or until it is nicely browned.

4. Transfer the okra to a metal baking dish such as a cake pan and place it on the top rack of the grill. Cook over low heat, stirring occasionally, for about 10 minutes more or until the okra is well cooked.

Excalibur Potatoes

*Thin slices of potato are cooked on the grill
and coated with a savory seasoning.*

Yield: 4 servings
Time: 10 minutes to prepare
5–7 minutes to cook

4 medium potatoes
1 tablespoon oil
1/4 cup nutritional yeast
2 teaspoons onion powder
1/2 teaspoon sea salt
1 teaspoon paprika
pinch of cayenne

1. Scrub the potatoes—do not peel them— and cut out any bad spots. Slice them into very thin slices (between 1/8 and 1/4-inch thick).

2. Brush the potatoes very lightly with oil. Place the potato slices on the bottom rack of the grill. Cook over low heat until they are brown on the bottom, 3–4 minutes. Turn them over and cook until they are tender (about 3 minutes more). Transfer to a large bowl.

3. In a small bowl, combine the yeast, onion powder, salt, paprika, and cayenne. Mix well. Sprinkle this mixture over the potatoes and toss.

4. Serve immediately.

Serving Suggestion

These potatoes go well with Lancelot Tempeh (page 161), Camille's Combo (page 155), Seven Samurai Tofu (page 146), or just about any tofu, tempeh, or seitan dish.

El Cid Potatoes

The potato, probably native to the Andes,
was introduced into Spain in the Sixteenth Century.
Now, introduce it to your grill.

Yield: 4–6 servings

Time: 5 minutes to prepare

20–25 minutes to cook

---

2 pounds new potatoes, cut into halves
or quarters depending on size

1 tablespoon olive oil

1/2 teaspoon sea salt

1 teaspoon fresh rosemary or
1/2 teaspoon dry rosemary

10–12 large cloves garlic, peeled

1. Scrub the potatoes—do not peel—and cut out any bad spots. Cut the potatoes into bite-sized chunks and either steam or pressure cook until the chunks are just barely tender.

2. Place the lightly cooked potatoes in a mixing bowl. Add the olive oil, salt, and rosemary. Mix well. Place a rack with small holes over the bottom rack of your grill. Place the potatoes on the rack and cook over medium heat until they are browned all over (approximately 5 minutes). Turn them as necessary so that they brown evenly. Place the roasted potatoes in a serving bowl and keep them warm.

3. Place the garlic in a small metal pan or on a sheet of aluminum foil. Place on the top rack of the grill and cook over low heat, turning often, until the cloves are tender and brown (5–10 minutes). Remove the garlic cloves from the grill and slice them into slivers. Top the potatoes with the roasted garlic.

4. Serve immediately.

Joie de Vivre Baked Potatoes

These potatoes are so delicious,
you won't be tempted to add butter or sour cream.

Yield: 2 servings
Time: 5 minutes to prepare
60 minutes to cook

2 baking potatoes
2 tablespoons olive oil
2 tablespoons tamari
2 cloves garlic
1 teaspoon herbes de Provence

1. Scrub the potatoes—do not peel— and cut out any bad spots. Place the potatoes on a cutting board and make a series of 1/2-inch thick slices in each potato, without cutting all the way through to the bottom. (An easy way to do this is to place a wooden spoon on the cutting board alongside of the potato. Cut into the potato until the knife rests on the spoon. The spoon will stop the knife from going all the way through.)

2. In a small bowl, mix together the olive oil, tamari, garlic, and herbs.

3. Place each potato on a sheet of aluminum foil. Using a brush or a spoon, coat the top of each potato and the inside of the slices with the oil mixture. Any leftover mixture can be drizzled over the top. Wrap the potatoes in the foil, place them on the top rack of the grill, and cook over low heat for about 1 hour or until a fork can easily pierce the potatoes.

Scarlet's Sweet Potatoes

*Sweet potatoes are as Southern as Scarlet O'Hara
and wonderful cooked on a grill.*

Yield: 8 servings (1 medium potato per person)
Time: 5 minutes to prepare
35 minutes to cook

8 medium-sized potatoes

1. Scrub the potatoes—do not peel—and cut out any bad spots. With a fork, pierce the skin of each potato in a few places. Wrap each potato in aluminum foil. Place the potatoes on the top rack of your grill and cook over low heat for about 35 minutes or until a fork can easily be inserted into the potato. Turn the potatoes occasionally and move them around on the rack because the potatoes in the center of the grill tend to cook faster than those around the outside.

2. If the potato skin becomes burnt, remove it before serving.

Serving Suggestion

Serve the potatoes plain to accompany a tofu or tempeh dish, or try them with Caprice Cashew Sauce (page 76) and a green salad.

Strange Bedfellows

If you like garlic and you like sweet potatoes, you'll love these garlicky sweet-potato slices!

Yield: 4 servings
Time: 10 minutes to prepare
10–15 minutes to cook

2 medium sweet potatoes
1 tablespoon oil
3 cloves garlic, pressed
1 tablespoon tamari

1. Scrub the potatoes—do not peel—cut out any bad spots, and slice into thin rounds.

2. In a mixing bowl, combine the oil, garlic, and tamari. Mix well and add the sweet potatoes. Stir again to coat the sweet potatoes with the mixture. Place the sweet potatoes on the grill. Cook over low heat until the potatoes are brown on the bottom (about 5 minutes). Turn them over and cook on the other side. (If the potatoes start to burn before they are tender, either transfer to the top rack the potato slices that are cooking too quickly, or turn off one burner and transfer the potatoes to that side for a few minutes.) Then, turn the burner back on and finish cooking the potatoes for 5–10 minutes.

Don Quixote Mushrooms and Onions

*Grilled mushrooms have a different texture and flavor
than sautéed mushrooms.*

Yield: 4–6 servings
Time: 15 minutes to prepare
10 minutes to grill

3 cups whole, medium-sized mushrooms
*2 cups onions, sliced into rounds
that are then cut in half*
1 tablespoon olive oil
2 tablespoons tamari
6 cloves garlic, pressed

1. Wash and dry the mushrooms. Place them in a large bowl. Add the onions. Set aside.

2. In a small bowl, mix together the oil, tamari, and garlic. Pour this mixture over the mushrooms and onions. Mix well and let sit for 10 minutes. Place a rack with small holes over the bottom rack of your grill and place the mushroom/onion mixture on the rack. Grill over low heat, stirring often, for about 10 minutes or until the onions are tender and lightly browned.

3. Serve immediately.

Serving Suggestion

Grilled mushrooms and onions are a wonderful accompaniment to grilled tofu, tempeh, or seitan dishes.

Sixth Happiness

*In Southern Italy, young zucchini are boiled together
with the flowers and leaves of the zucchini plant
and sautéed with garlic. Zucchini can also be given
an Oriental flavor and be prepared quickly and easily
on your grill.*

Yield: 3–4 servings
Time: 5 minutes to prepare
5 minutes to cook

2–3 medium zucchini
2 teaspoons grated fresh ginger, approximately
1 teaspoon toasted sesame oil
1 teaspoon oil
2 teaspoons tamari
2 cloves garlic, pressed

1. Wash the zucchini well and cut them into thin lengthwise slices.

2. Grate about 2 teaspoons of fresh ginger and, with your hand, squeeze it into a teaspoon to measure it. Use enough ginger to yield 1 teaspoon of ginger juice.

3. In a small bowl, combine the remaining ingredients. Brush this mixture over the top of the zucchini slices. Place the slices on the grill, brushed side down. Brush the tops with the remaining oil/seasoning mixture. Cook for about 3 minutes or until the zucchini are lightly browned on the bottom. Turn them over and cook for about 2 minutes more, or until tender.

4. Serve immediately.

Serving Suggestion

Serve Sixth Happiness with grain dishes or with grilled tofu, seitan, or tempeh dishes.

Garden Grill

You can enjoy mixed vegetables hot off the grill!

Yield: 4 servings

Time: 10 minutes to prepare

10–13 minutes to cook

*1 1/2 cups thinly sliced and quartered
sweet onion*

*1 medium-sized zucchini,
cut into 1/4-inch-thick rounds*

*1 medium yellow squash,
cut into 1/4-inch-thick rounds*

1 green pepper, diced

*2 cups sliced, medium-sized mushrooms or
whole small mushrooms*

1 teaspoon herbes de Provence

1 tablespoon tamari

1 tablespoon olive oil

12 cherry tomatoes

1. In a large bowl, mix together all the ingredients, except for the cherry tomatoes. Place a rack with small holes over the bottom rack of your grill. Place the mixed vegetables on the rack. Cook over low heat, stirring constantly, until the vegetables are almost tender (about 10 minutes).

2. Add the cherry tomatoes and cook for 2–3 minutes more.

Serving Suggestion

Garden Grill is good with tofu or tempeh dishes, or with Poca-hontas's Polenta (page 101) and Madonna Sauce (page 81).

Seventh Heaven Kebobs

In Turkish, "shish" means "skewer" and "kebap" means "roast meat." Try these kebobs instead. They're light and nutritious and much prettier than meat.

Yield: 4–8 servings (8 kebobs)
Time: 1 hour to soak bamboo skewers
20 minutes to prepare
15 minutes to cook

8 bamboo skewers
1 Spanish onion, cut into 1-inch chunks
water sufficient to steam onion
1 head broccoli, separated into flowerettes
1 head cauliflower, separated into flowerettes
16 cherry tomatoes
16 medium-sized mushrooms
1 medium-large zucchini, cut into 1-inch cubes
2 tablespoons olive oil
1 tablespoon vegetable bouillon powder
1/2 teaspoon herbes de Provence
1/4 teaspoon sea salt

1. Soak 8 bamboo skewers for at least 1 hour before grilling.

2. Place the onion in a vegetable steamer. Place the steamer in a large pot with 1/2-inch of water in the bottom. Cover the pot and bring the water to a boil. Reduce the heat and steam the onion for about 2 minutes. Add the cauliflower and the broccoli flowerettes to the steamer and cook for about 2 minutes more.

3. Thread the lightly steamed and the remaining raw vegetables onto the skewers, alternating the type of vegetable, until you fill the 8 skewers.

4. In a small bowl, combine the olive oil, vegetable bouillon powder, herbs, and salt. Lightly brush the vegetables with this mixture. Place a rack with small holes over the bottom rack of

your grill. Place the kebobs on the grill and cook, over low heat, turning as needed for about 10 minutes or until the vegetables are tender. Do not overcook.

Serving Suggestion

Serve the kebobs over a bed of brown rice or pasta with your favorite sauce. The Teriyaki Sauce (page 87) would be good, as would the Dionysian Dill Sauce (page 77), Madonna Sauce (page 81), or Caprice Cashew Sauce (page 76).

Intermezzo

Known long ago as "love apples," tomatoes can be grilled for a quick and easy side dish.

Yield: 4–6 servings
Time: 5 minutes to prepare
5–8 minutes to cook

4 large tomatoes
2 teaspoons olive oil
1/4 teaspoon sea salt
1 teaspoon basil

1. Wash the tomatoes and cut them into 1/2-inch slices.

2. Brush the tomato slices lightly with oil. Place the tomato slices on the bottom rack of your grill over medium heat. Cook for 3–5 minutes. Turn them over and cook for 2–3 minutes more.

Serving Suggestion

Grilled tomatoes are divine when served with Pesto de Venus (page 80) as an appetizer or a side dish. If you are going to add the pesto, do not sprinkle the tomatoes with salt and basil.

Vegetables Robusto

To many people, Italian cooking is synonymous with the use of garlic. But garlic was originally cultivated in China, then used in Egypt, then introduced to the Romans.

Yield: 6 servings
Time: 20 minutes to prepare
20–25 minutes to cook

Dressing

2 tablespoons olive oil

2 tablespoons balsamic vinegar

5 cloves garlic, pressed

1 teaspoon oregano

1/2 teaspoon sea salt

Vegetables

*2 medium-sized eggplants
(about 3/4 pound each)*

3 medium-sized yellow squash (about 1 pound)

4 Italian plum tomatoes, sliced

1 large green pepper, seeded and cut into strips

3 cups mushrooms, cut into halves

1. In a small bowl, combine the oil, vinegar, garlic, oregano, and salt. Mix well.

2. Cut the eggplant into 1/2-inch-thick lengthwise strips. Cut the squash into lengthwise strips that are slightly thinner than the eggplant strips.

3. Brush the eggplant, squash, and tomatoes with the dressing. Place the eggplant slices on the bottom rack of your grill and cook over low heat until they are brown on the bottom (about 5 minutes). Turn them over and cook them on the other side. Remove the slices to a serving platter.

4. Repeat step 3 using the squash.

5. Place the tomato slices on the grill and cook them for about 3 minutes on one side. Place them on the serving platter over the squash and eggplant slices.

6. If there is any leftover dressing, pour it over the mushrooms and green peppers. Mix well. (If there is no leftover dressing, the peppers and mushrooms can cook without it.) Place a rack with small holes over the bottom rack of your grill. Place the mushrooms and peppers on the rack and cook, stirring occasionally, until they are tender (about 5 minutes).

7. Arrange the mushrooms and peppers on the serving platter over the other vegetables. Serve warm, at room temperature, or chilled.

Gary Cooper Corn

On a campfire or a gas grill,
corn on the cob is easy and, oh, so good!

Yield: 8 servings (1 ear per person)
Time: About 10 minutes to prepare
About 10 minutes to cook

8 ears of corn, with husks
water sufficient to soak corn

1. Choose fresh corn that has not been husked. Pull back the leaves on each ear of corn and wash away the silks. Fold the leaves back over the ears so that they cover the corn.

2. Place the corn in a sink or large bowl and cover with water. Let the corn soak for about 5 minutes.

3. Place the corn in the husk directly on the bottom rack of the grill and cook over low heat for about 10 minutes, turning often.

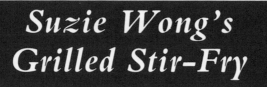

Suzie Wong's Grilled Stir-Fry

These "stir-fried" vegetables have a grilled flavor and an Oriental sauce.

Yield: 4–5 servings
Time: 10 minutes to prepare
15–20 minutes to cook

Sauce

1 tablespoon finely grated fresh ginger
1 cup water
3 cloves garlic, pressed
2 tablespoons tamari
1 tablespoon honey
1 tablespoon arrowroot

Vegetables

2 cups thinly sliced onions
1 large red bell pepper, sliced
1 teaspoon oil
1 1/4 pounds mushrooms, sliced
1 tablespoon oil
1/2 pound snow peas, cleaned
8 large leaves Chinese cabbage, chopped
1 teaspoon oil

1. In a small bowl, combine the ginger, water, garlic, tamari, honey, and arrowroot. Mix well and set aside.

2. In a large bowl, combine the onions, pepper, and 1 teaspoon of oil. Mix well to coat the vegetables with the oil. Place a rack

with small holes or a "wok topper" over the bottom rack of your grill. Place the vegetables on the rack and cook over medium heat, stirring constantly, for 3–4 minutes. Reduce the flame to low, cover the grill, and cook the vegetables for 1–2 minutes more. They should be just barely tender but still crisp. If not, continue to cook and stir for a couple of minutes more. Transfer vegetables to a large pan.

3. Place the mushrooms in the bowl. Add the tablespoon of oil and mix well. Place the mushrooms on the grill over medium heat and cook, stirring constantly, until they are browned (about 4–5 minutes). Add them to the pan with the other vegetables.

4. Place the snow peas and cabbage in a bowl. Add the remaining teaspoon of oil and mix well. Place the vegetables on the bottom rack of the grill and cook over medium heat, stirring constantly, for 2–3 minutes. Reduce the flame to low and cover the grill. Cook for about 1 minute more. If the vegetables are just barely tender, add them to the pan with the other vegetables. If not, stir and cook for about 1 minute more.

5. Stir the sauce and add it to the pan with the vegetables. Bring it to a boil and remove it from the heat.

6. Serve immediately.

Serving Suggestion

Serve over brown rice or whole-grain noodles and feature as a side dish with Hesperides Tempeh (page 144), Temptress Tofu (page 141), or The Joy of Tofu (page 143).

Autumn Bouquet

*Hearty root vegetables simmered on the grill
are perfect for a beautiful autumn evening.*

Yield: 4–6 servings

Time: About 15 minutes to prepare

20–30 minutes to cook

1/2 medium-sized cabbage, chopped

*1 large or 2 medium-sized carrots,
scrubbed and sliced*

1 large turnip, scrubbed and cubed

2 medium parsnips, scrubbed and sliced

1 sweet potato, scrubbed and cubed

1 celery root, peeled and diced

2 tablespoons olive oil

4 bay leaves

1 tablespoon herbes de Provence

1 teaspoon sea salt

1. Place all the vegetables on a large sheet of aluminum foil. Drizzle the olive oil over the vegetables and distribute the 4 bay leaves throughout the mixture. Sprinkle with the herbs and salt.

2. Fold the foil over the vegetables and close it to make a package. Place the package of vegetables on the top rack of the grill and cook over medium-low heat for 20–30 minutes or until the vegetables are tender. After about 15 minutes, check the vegetables and stir them. Reclose the package and cook until the vegetables are tender. (You can cook a second dish on the grill and keep the vegetable package closed so it will stay warm for a long time.)

Serving Suggestion

This symphony of vitamins harmonizes beautifully with the Anna Karenina Stroganoff (page 163).

Achy Breaky Beans

Baked beans are the classic country and western food,
but traditionally they are made with lots of sugar,
which makes them very difficult to digest.
In this recipe, the beans' sweetness comes from the spices
and from slowly cooking the onion.

Yield: 4 servings
Time: Soak the beans overnight
10 minutes to prepare
1 hour, 20 minutes to cook

1 cup dry great northern beans
2 1/2 cups water
2 tablespoons olive oil
1 large Spanish onion, sliced
5–6 cloves garlic, finely chopped
1 teaspoon cinnamon
1/2 teaspoon allspice
3 tablespoons natto miso
1/4 cup tomato paste

1. Wash and pick through the beans. Place them in a bowl and let them soak for 8–10 hours.

2. Drain and rinse the beans. Place them in a large pot and add the water. Bring to a boil, cover, and reduce the heat. Simmer, stirring occasionally, for about 1 hour or more until the beans are very tender.

3. While the beans are cooking, heat the oil in a skillet and add the sliced onion and the garlic. Sauté over low heat for 30 minutes, stirring occasionally.

4. When the beans are tender, add the onions and the remaining ingredients. Mix well, and transfer to an oiled metal baking dish. Cover the dish with aluminum foil and place it on the top rack of the grill. Cook over medium-low heat for 15 minutes or until the beans are thick and bubbly hot.

Ophelia's Onions

We knew that these were good when a 10-year-old girl asked for seconds.

Yield: 4–8 servings
Time: 10 minutes to prepare
About 30 minutes to cook

4 large Spanish onions
1 tablespoon olive oil
2 cups finely chopped mushrooms
1/4 cup TVP
2 cups whole-grain bread crumbs
1 teaspoon herbes de Provence
2 tablespoons tamari
1/4 cup water + water sufficient to cover bottom of baking dish

1. Peel the onions and cut them in half lengthwise. Using a sharp paring knife, cut away enough of the inside of each onion to leave a shell that is about 3/4-inch thick.

2. Heat the oil in a skillet and add the mushrooms. Sauté for 3–4 minutes, then add the TVP, the bread crumbs, and the herbs.

3. In a small bowl, mix together the tamari and 1/4 cup water. Pour this mixture over the mushroom mixture in the skillet. Mix well.

4. Fill the onion shells with the mushroom mixture, packing them well.

5. Place the onions in a metal baking dish (such as a cake pan). Pour about 1/4-inch of water into the bottom of the dish and cover with aluminum foil. Place the stuffed onions on the top rack of your grill and cook over low heat for about 25 minutes or until the onion shell is tender. Check the onions occasionally to make sure that they don't get over-cooked.

6. If desired, carefully remove the onions from their pan, brush

them with oil, and place them on the bottom rack of the grill for 3–4 minutes to brown them.

Serving Suggestion

Add grilled potatoes and a big salad and enjoy.

Rites of Spring Asparagus

It is easy to cook asparagus "au point" on a grill.

Yield: 4 servings
Time: 5 minutes to prepare
3–4 minutes to cook

1 pound fresh asparagus
1 tablespoon olive oil, or less as needed
1/4 teaspoon sea salt.

1. Wash the asparagus well and snap off the tough ends.

2. In a small bowl, mix together the oil and the salt. Lightly brush the asparagus with this mixture. Place the asparagus on the bottom rack of your grill over medium-low heat. Cook for about 3–4 minutes or until tender but still crisp. Turn the asparagus often as they cook and be careful not to burn them.

Serving Suggestion

Grilled asparagus is delicious plain, with Dionysian Dill Sauce (page 77), or with Balm of Gilead (page 78).

Geisha Delight

These kebobs get much of their Oriental flavor
from ginger, which was brought to Southern Europe from
the Orient before the establishment of the Roman Empire.

Yield: 8 kebobs

Time: 1 hour to marinate tofu and soak skewers

15 minutes to prepare

About 15 minutes to cook

Marinade

2 tablespoons tamari
1 tablespoon toasted sesame oil
1 tablespoon finely grated fresh ginger
2 cloves garlic, pressed

Kebobs

1 pound tofu
1/2 Spanish onion, cut into 1-inch cubes
16 medium-sized mushrooms, cleaned
3 large leaves Chinese cabbage,
cut into 1-inch-wide strips
1 large red pepper, cut into 1-inch cubes
1 tablespoon oil, or as needed

1. Cover the bamboo skewers with water and let them soak for 1 hour.

2. In a shallow container such as a cake pan, combine the marinade ingredients. Mix well.

3. Cut the tofu into 1 1/2-inch cubes and place them in the pan with the marinade. Let sit for 1 hour or more, turning the tofu occasionally. (The tofu can marinate all day if you wish, but place it in the refrigerator if it is going to marinate for more than 2 hours.)

4. Steam the onions for 3–4 minutes or until they are just starting to become tender.

5. Alternately thread tofu and vegetables onto bamboo skewers. Brush the kebobs with oil and place them on the bottom rack of the grill. Cook over low heat, turning often, for about 10 minutes or until tofu is grilled and vegetables are just tender.

Serving Suggestion

Serve over a bed of brown rice with Teriyaki Sauce (page 87) or with Seduction Salad (page 69).

Madame Bovary's Beets

Beets cooked this way are especially sweet and flavorful.

Yield: 8 servings (1 large beet for 2 persons)
Time: 5 minutes to prepare
35–45 minutes to cook

4 large beets

1. Scrub the beets well. Don't peel them but cut a slice off of the stem end and the root end.

2. Wrap each beet in a sheet of aluminum foil and place the beets on the top rack of the grill. Cook over low heat for 35–45 minutes or until the beets can be easily pierced with a fork. Turn the beets occasionally as they cook and move them around on the grill because the beets in the center of the grill tend to cook faster than those around the edges.

3. When the beets are tender, remove them from the grill and peel any with charred skin.

Serving Suggestion

Slice the beets and serve them plain or with a little olive oil, lemon, and seasoned salt.

Main Dishes

Grilling is a delicious way to introduce healthy vegetarian foods to nonvegetarians. The wonderful flavor that comes only from grilling is something that everyone loves. Even people who claim not to like tofu may enjoy Seven Samurai Tofu (page 146). High-protein kebobs, made with tempeh or seitan, and hearty stews with a subtle grilled flavor are so good that it's hard to believe they are good for you.

Different types of veggie burgers and croquettes served with a light, tasty sauce and accompanied by rice or whole-grain bread and vegetables make a lovely meal. Grilled stuffed vegetables or a vegetable curry with fresh chutney are equally lovely.

Most of the following recipes have serving suggestions, which are, by no means, the only ways to serve them. Be creative; serve these main dishes however they appeal to you. But don't forget the importance of a beautiful presentation. Make a dish of seitan and potatoes much prettier by decorating the plate with brightly colored vegetables. A spiral slice of fresh orange will liven up Hesperides Tempeh (page 144), and branches of fresh herbs, or leaves of tender greens will make almost any dish more attractive.

The main thing to remember when preparing these recipes, as with all grill recipes, is to watch the food as it cooks. The grill is hot and foods can burn easily. Stay with the grill, turn the food as it cooks, and move it around on the grill if there are hot spots.

Grilling adds a festive quality to vegetarian main dishes, which makes them ideal for entertaining. Dominique and I and all of our guests have really enjoyed these recipes and we hope that you will, too.

VEGETARIAN FAST FOODS ON THE GRILL

Even when you are too busy for gourmet cooking, the availability of prepared foods makes it possible to enjoy cooking out. Tempeh burgers, veggie burgers, and tofu hot dogs are the best prepared foods for grilling. All of these products taste good to begin with, but when they are grilled and served with the right garnishes, they are great! Many different brands of burgers and hot dogs are sold, but we prefer Yves Veggie Cuisine Burgers and dogs.

Burgers

Tempeh burgers are made from precooked and seasoned tempeh. Yves Veggie Burgers are made with grains, vegetables, wheat and soy proteins, and seasonings. To grill any kind of vegetarian burger, just brush each side of the burger very lightly with oil and cook the burger on the bottom rack of the grill over low heat until it is nicely browned. Tempeh burgers should be cooked about 4–5 minutes on each side or until they are browned, but Yves Burgers cook faster (about 2–3 minutes on each side).

All types of veggie burgers are wonderful with the Whole-Wheat Burger Buns on page 181, or with any whole-wheat bun, or even on whole-grain English muffins. Garnish the burgers just as you would hamburgers, with slices of grilled onion, tomato, pickle, catsup, and mustard, or be creative and garnish them with sliced avocado, sprouts, soy cheese, raw spinach, watercress, arugula, etc. Also try them with some of the homemade relishes in this book. Garden of Delights Relish on page 86 is especially good with burgers.

Tofu Wieners

Tofu hot dogs taste so much like the real thing that some vegetarians don't like to eat them. Once, Vicki served tofu dogs at a party; a nonvegetarian neighbor who ate one asked why a vegetarian would serve hot dogs. He didn't have a clue that he was not eating meat!

To grill tofu hot dogs, first boil them, half covered with water, for 2–3 minutes and then place them directly on the bottom rack of your grill over medium-low heat. Cook, turning them often, until they are hot and lightly grilled (about 3 minutes).

What makes the hot dogs really good is some homemade relish. Try Reveler's Relish on page 84 and Melodious Maize on page 85. They are delicious. Other garnishes for tofu dogs are vegetarian chili, sauerkraut, and, of course, mustard. To make these dogs extra-special, serve them on homemade buns (page 181).

Bogey's Burgers

Our favorite burgers are made with eggplant.

Yield: 4 servings (about 8 burgers)
Time: 30 minutes to prepare
(includes 20 minutes for eggplant to set)
20 minutes to grill

1 medium-large eggplant (1 1/4–1 1/2 pounds)
1 tablespoon olive oil, or as needed
2 tablespoons tamari
1/4 cup dry onion flakes
10 sun-dried tomato halves,
snipped into small pieces with scissors
1 cup TVP
1 teaspoon thyme
1/4 teaspoon celery seeds
1/2 teaspoon oregano
2 cloves garlic, pressed
3 tablespoons tahini
1 tablespoon oil
1 teaspoon liquid smoke

1. Wash the eggplant and cut into 1/2-inch-thick rounds. Lightly brush the slices on both sides with oil (approximately 1 tablespoon). Grill the eggplant over low heat until it is brown on the bottom (about 5 minutes). Turn it over and cook the other side (about 5 minutes).

2. Place the eggplant in a food processor with the tamari and blend to a purée.

3. Transfer the eggplant purée to a mixing bowl and add the dry onion flakes, tomato pieces, TVP, thyme, celery seeds, oregano, garlic, and tahini. Let the mixture set, covered, for about 20 minutes.

4. Shape the mixture into patties that are about 4 inches in diameter and a little over 1/2-inch thick.

5. In a small bowl, combine the remaining tablespoon of oil with the liquid smoke. Brush this mixture over the patties. Place the patties on the grill and cook over low heat until they are brown on the bottom (4–5 minutes). Turn them over and cook the other side (4–5 minutes).

Serving Suggestion

These burgers are delicious on toasted whole-grain English muffins or burger buns, garnished with mustard, tomato, and lettuce. They are also good plain or with a tomato sauce.

Bacall Burgers

We've put a modern twist on lentils and used them in vegetarian burgers. The peanut butter holds the burgers together. Don't laugh; they're really delicious.

Yield: 4 servings (about 12 patties)
Time: 1 hour to prepare
(includes time to cook lentils and 15 minutes sitting time)
About 8 minutes to grill

1 cup dry green lentils
2 cups water
1/4 cup dry onion flakes
15 sun-dried tomato halves, ground in a blender
2 tablespoons tamari
1/2 teaspoon thyme
1/2 teaspoon sage
2 tablespoons peanut butter, chunky or smooth
1 1/2 tablespoons oil
1 teaspoon liquid smoke

1. Wash and pick over the lentils. Place them in a heavy, medium-sized pan with the water. Cover and bring the water to a boil. Reduce the heat and simmer over low for about 45 minutes or until the lentils are very tender and all the water is absorbed.

2. Place the cooked lentils in a mixing bowl. Add the onion flakes, ground sun-dried tomatoes, tamari, thyme, and sage. Let sit for about 15 minutes so the dried vegetables absorb the liquid from the tamari and the lentils.

3. Add the peanut butter and mix well, using your hands. Shape the mixture into approximately 12 small patties that are about 2 1/4 inches in diameter and about 1-inch thick.

4. In a cup or small bowl, combine the oil and the liquid smoke. Brush this mixture over the patties. Place the patties on the bottom rack of the grill and cook over low heat until they are brown on the bottom (4–5 minutes). Turn them over and cook until they are brown on the other side (4–5 minutes).

Serving Suggestion

These patties are good with Kamasutra Curry (page 150). They are also good with brown rice, a grilled vegetable, and a tomato sauce.

African Queen Croquettes

*Teff, a versatile and delicious grain, is a staple of
the Ethiopian diet. Mix it with vegetables to make these
croquettes, and you've a combination as memorable as
Bogey and Hepburn in African Queen.*

Yield: 3–6 servings (6 patties)
Time: 45 minutes to prepare
(includes 30 minutes cooling time)
About 10 minutes to grill

1 cup teff

3 cups water

1 teaspoon thyme

15 sun-dried tomato halves

1/3 cup finely chopped bell pepper

1/3 cup grated carrots

1/3 cup finely chopped celery

1/3 cup finely chopped onion

2 cloves garlic, pressed

1/2 teaspoon sea salt

1 teaspoon cumin

2 tablespoons oil

1 tablespoon tamari

1/2 teaspoon liquid smoke

1. In a heavy, medium-sized pan combine the teff, water, and thyme. Bring the mixture to a boil, cover, and reduce the heat. Simmer over low heat, stirring occasionally, for 15 minutes or until the teff is very thick. While the teff is cooking, prepare the vegetables.

2. Place the sun-dried tomatoes in a blender and grind them into small pieces. Add the tomatoes to the hot teff mixture. Add

the pepper, carrots, celery, onion, garlic, salt, and cumin. Let the mixture set, uncovered, until it is cool enough to handle (about 15 minutes).

3. When the teff is cool enough to touch but still warm, shape the mixture into 6 patties that are about 3 inches in diameter and 1-inch thick. Place the patties on a cookie sheet and put the sheet in the refrigerator for 15–30 minutes. The patties will become firmer as they cool.

4. In a small bowl, combine the oil, tamari, and liquid smoke. Brush this mixture generously over the tops of the patties. Place a rack with small holes over the bottom rack of your grill. Brush the rack lightly with oil. Place the patties, oiled side down, on the rack and cook over medium heat for about 5 minutes or until they are crispy brown on the bottom. Brush the tops of the patties with the oil mixture and turn them over. Cook until the tops are brown and crispy (about 5 minutes).

Serving Suggestion

These patties are delicious plain or with Madonna Sauce (page 81). You can also enjoy them with Caprice Cashew Sauce (page 76) or Dionysian Dill Sauce (page 77).

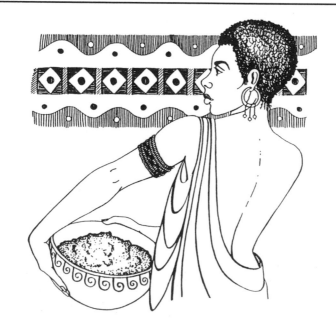

Cupid Croquettes

*You're bound to love the flavor and texture
of these croquettes. Some people call quinoa
"vegetarian caviar" because it has a similar texture.*

Yield: 4–6 servings (12 patties)

Time: 30 minutes to prepare

10 minutes to grill

*1 cup quinoa
2 cups water
1/2 pound tempeh, thawed if frozen
water sufficient to steam tempeh
1/3 cup finely chopped onion
1/4 cup tahini
2 cloves garlic, pressed
2 tablespoons tamari
1/2 teaspoon sage
1/2 teaspoon oregano
2 tablespoons nutritional yeast
2 tablespoons oil*

1. Place the quinoa in a medium-sized pan. Add enough water to wash the qrain. Swish it around with your hand to wash it. Drain through a fine wire strainer and return the quinoa to the pan. Add two cups of water. Cover the pan and bring the water to a boil. Reduce the heat and simmer over low heat until the water is absorbed (15–20 minutes).

2. Cut the tempeh into cubes and place in a vegetable steamer. Place the steamer in a large pan with about 1 inch of water in the bottom. Cover the pan and bring the water to a boil. Reduce the heat to a simmer and steam the tempeh for about 10 minutes.

3. Transfer the tempeh to a mixing bowl. Mash it with a fork. Add the cooked quinoa, onion, tahini, garlic, tamari, sage, oregano, and yeast. Mix well.

4. Using your hands, shape the mixture into 12 patties that are about 2 1/2 inches in diameter and about 3/4-inch thick.

5. Place a rack with small holes over the bottom rack of your grill. Brush the top of the patties with oil and place them on the rack with the oiled side down. Cook them over low heat for about 5 minutes or until they are brown on the bottom. Brush the top of the patties with the remaining oil and turn them over. Cook until they are brown.

Serving Suggestion

Serve Cupid Croquettes with a sauce (it's delicious with Sarong Sauce on page 73) or with your favorite relish.

Temptress Tofu

Even people who say that they don't like tofu,
like it when it is well-seasoned and grilled.

Yield: 3–4 servings
Time: 20 minutes to prepare
1 hour to marinate
About 10 minutes to grill

1 pound firm tofu
1/3 cup lemon or lime juice
1 tablespoon toasted sesame oil
2–3 tablespoons tamari, to taste
2 tablespoons grated onion
1 teaspoon tarragon
1 tablespoon oil

1. Cut the tofu into fish-stick-size pieces (about 1 inch x 3 inches x 1/2 inch).

2. In a small bowl, combine the lemon or lime juice, toasted sesame oil, tamari, onion, and tarragon.

3. Pour this mixture over the tofu, and let it marinate for about 1 hour. Turn the tofu over occasionally to make sure that it is completely covered with the marinade.

4. Brush the tops of the tofu pieces lightly with oil and place them on the bottom rack of your grill, oiled side down. Cook over low heat until the pieces are browned and crispy on the bottom (about 5 minutes). If there is any leftover marinating liquid, brush it over the tofu as it cooks. Brush the tops with the remaining oil and turn the tofu over. Cook until browned and crispy on the bottom (about 5 minutes).

Serving Suggestion

Tofu prepared this way is delicious plain or with your favorite

BBQ sauce. For a great sandwich, try Temptress Tofu on whole-wheat buns (page 181) with a BBQ sauce, lettuce, and tomato. It is also good served with rice and vegetable dishes.

Indonesian Delight

Spicy peanut sauce and sweet grilled pineapple bring a taste of Indonesia to your back yard.

Yield: 6 servings

Time: About 35 minutes to prepare

15 minutes to grill

2 cups diced red onion

4 medium carrots, sliced

1/2 fresh pineapple, peeled, cored, and cut into 1-inch cubes

1 tablespoon oil

1 bunch broccoli

1 recipe Siam Sauce (page 79)

1. Place the onion, carrots, and pineapple on a large sheet of aluminum foil. Drizzle with the oil and mix well, being careful not to tear the aluminum. Fold the aluminum to form a package. Place the package of vegetables on the bottom rack of your grill over low heat for about 5 minutes.

2. While the vegetables are cooking, wash the broccoli and cut the flowerettes into bite-sized pieces. Reserve the stems for soups.

3. Carefully open the package of vegetables and add the broccoli. Mix well. Close the package and cook about 10 minutes or until the vegetables are tender but still slightly crisp.

4. While the vegetables are cooking, make the sauce.

5. Place the vegetables over a bed of long-grain brown rice and top with the sauce. Serve immediately.

The Joy of Tofu

When time is tight but you refuse to skimp on taste,
this dish is just the thing.

Yield: 3–4 servings
Time: 10 minutes to prepare
10 minutes to grill

1 pound firm tofu
2 tablespoons + 1 teaspoon tamari
1 teaspoon roasted sesame oil
1 tablespoon honey
1 teaspoon liquid smoke
3 cloves garlic, pressed
1–2 tablespoons oil, as needed

1. Cut the tofu into 1/4-inch-thick slices.

2. In a small bowl, combine the tamari, sesame oil, honey, liquid smoke, and garlic. Mix well.

3. Brush both sides of the tofu slices with this mixture and set the mixture aside. Brush the tofu lightly with oil. Place the tofu on the bottom rack of your grill. Cook it over low heat until it is nicely browned on the bottom (about 5 minutes). Brush the tops with leftover oil and turn the slices over. Brush the tops with any leftover tamari mixture. Cook until the bottoms are nicely browned. Turn the tofu slices over very briefly, brush with any remaining sauce, and remove from the grill.

Serving Suggestion

Serve the tofu with grilled vegetables over a bed of brown rice. Add your choice of BBQ sauce. The Joy of Tofu is also very good in sandwiches.

Hesperides Tempeh

Combine sesame with the flavor of oranges—
once identified with the golden apples that grew
in the garden of the Hesperides—and you've got a dish
that is as exotic as it is tasty.

Yield: 4–5 servings
Time: 20 minutes to prepare
3–4 minutes to grill

1 pound tempeh (2 packages of 8 ounces each),
thawed if frozen
water sufficient to steam tempeh
1 tablespoon tamari
1/2 cup fruit-sweetened orange marmalade
1 tablespoon balsamic vinegar
1 tablespoon toasted sesame oil
1 tablespoon sesame seeds
1 tablespoon tamari, approximately
1 tablespoon oil, approximately

1. Cut each 1/2-pound slab of tempeh into 8 pieces. (If you cut each slab as you would a pie, the pieces of tempeh will have a nice triangular shape.)

2. Place the pieces of tempeh in a vegetable steamer. Place the steamer in a pot with about 1 inch of water in the bottom and bring the water to a boil. Reduce the heat to medium-low and let the tempeh steam for about 10 minutes. Remove the tempeh from the steamer and let it cool for 5–10 minutes, or until it is cool enough to handle.

3. While the tempeh is cooling, make the sauce. In a small mixing bowl, combine 1 tablespoon tamari, the marmalade, vinegar, toasted sesame oil, and sesame seeds. Mix well and set aside.

4. Place the remaining tablespoon of tamari in a small bowl or cup. Brush the tempeh lightly on both sides with the tamari. Use a little more if necessary to cover the tempeh. Then brush the tempeh lightly with 1 tablespoon of oil, or as much as is needed to cover.

5. Cook the tempeh over low heat on the bottom rack of your grill until it is brown on the bottom (about 2 minutes). Turn it over and brush the grilled tops with the sauce. When the bottoms of the tempeh are browned, turn them over and brush the tops with the sauce. Let the tempeh cook for 1–2 minutes more. If desired, baste the tops of the tempeh pieces with more orange sauce as they cook. When the tempeh is shiny dark brown, it is done; do not let it burn.

Serving Suggestion

To serve, place the tempeh triangles around the edges of a platter and place a small bowl containing the leftover orange sauce in the center. This recipe is delicious with brown rice and Suzie Wong Grilled Stir-Fry (page 123).

Seven Samurai Tofu

Here's a tofu dish with a distinctly Western flavor.

Yield: 6 servings
Time: 20 minutes to prepare
20–33 minutes to grill

Tofu

1 tablespoon oil
3 cloves garlic, pressed
1 teaspoon liquid smoke
2 tablespoons tamari
2 pounds firm tofu, cut into bite-sized cubes
2 cups coarsely chopped onions
1 teaspoon oil
1 large green bell pepper, diced
1 teaspoon oil

Sauce

1 small can (5 1/2 ounces) tomato paste
1 tablespoon Dijon-style mustard
1/4 cup molasses
1–2 tablespoons tamari, to taste
3 cloves garlic, pressed
1/8 teaspoon cayenne
1/4 teaspoon allspice
1 1/2 tablespoons balsamic vinegar
1 cup water (approximately)

1. In a large mixing bowl, combine 1 tablespoon oil, garlic, liquid smoke, and tamari. Mix well.

2. Add the tofu cubes and mix again to coat the tofu with the mixture. Place a rack with small holes over the bottom rack of

your grill. Place the tofu on the rack and cook over low heat, turning as necessary until the tofu is brown and crispy all over (10–12 minutes). Set aside.

3. In a mixing bowl, combine the onions with 1 teaspoon of oil. Mix well to coat the onions. Place them on the rack and cook over low heat, stirring often, until tender (5–10 minutes). Set aside.

4. In a mixing bowl, combine the green pepper with 1 teaspoon of oil. Mix well. Place the pepper on the rack and cook over low heat, stirring often, until the pepper is tender (5–8 minutes). Set aside.

5. Now make the sauce: In a large kettle, combine the tomato paste, mustard, molasses, 1 tablespoon tamari, garlic, cayenne, allspice, and vinegar. Mix well. Add the tofu and the grilled vegetables. Mix again.

6. . Gradually stir in just enough water to give the sauce the desired consistency; don't add too much. Mix gently and bring the mixture to a simmer. Cook over low heat for 5–10 minutes so the flavors blend. Add a little more tamari, if desired, and thin with some water if the sauce gets too thick.

❧ *BARBECUE TIDBIT* ❧

It is a good idea, especially if you do a lot of entertaining, to buy an extra bottle of propane. If you run out of gas, it will probably be in the middle of a dinner party, like it was with us! On most grills, there is no way to know when the propane will run out, and if you have an extra bottle, you do not have to worry.

Instead of extra propane, you might buy one of two types of gauges for the propane bottle. One kind will accurately measure the remaining propane, but it costs about as much as a new bottle of propane. The less expensive one is not very accurate. ❑

South Seas Tempeh

*This colorful dish is defined by its sweet and sour sauce.
Traditionally, a sauce is a thickened liquid; in this case,
the thickener is arrowroot, which has an unobtrusive flavor
and imparts a delicate—almost fragile—texture to sauces.*

Yield: 4 servings

Time: About 10 minute to prepare

23–38 minutes to grill

---

*1/2 pound tempeh, thawed if frozen
and cut in bite-sized pieces*

water sufficient to steam tempeh

1 tablespoon tamari

1 tablespoon oil

1 cup coarsely chopped onion

1 teaspoon oil

1 red bell pepper, chopped

1 green bell pepper, chopped

1 teaspoon oil

2 cups fresh pineapple, in bite-sized pieces

1 cup snow peas, cleaned

1 teaspoon oil

Sauce

2 tablespoons mirin

1 tablespoon balsamic vinegar

1 tablespoon tamari, approximately

1 teaspoon freshly grated ginger

1 tablespoon honey

1 cup water

1 tablespoon arrowroot

1. Place the tempeh in a vegetable steamer with a little water in

the bottom of the pan. Cover, bring the water to a boil, then reduce the heat and steam the tempeh for about 10 minutes.

2. In a mixing bowl, combine 1 tablespoon tamari and 1 tablespoon oil. Add the steamed tempeh and mix gently to coat the tempeh with the mixture. Place a rack with small holes over the bottom rack of your grill. Place the tempeh on the grill over low heat and cook, turning often, until the tempeh is golden brown on all sides (5–8 minutes). Keep warm until needed.

3. Place the onion in a mixing bowl; add 1 teaspoon of oil and mix well to coat the onion with the oil. Place on the rack and cook over low heat until tender (about 5 minutes). Place in the bowl with the tempeh.

4. Combine the peppers with 1 teaspoon of oil. Mix to coat the peppers with the oil. Grill the peppers until tender (about 5 minutes). Add to the bowl with the tempeh and onions.

5. Mix the pineapple and the snow peas with 1 teaspoon oil. Grill over medium heat for 3–5 minutes. Add to the tempeh-vegetable mixture. Keep warm.

6. Now, make the sauce: In a saucepan, combine the mirin, vinegar, 1 tablespoon tamari, ginger, honey, water, and arrowroot. Mix well. While stirring constantly, bring the mixture to a boil.

7. Pour this mixture over the grilled vegetables and tempeh. Mix well. If desired, add a little more tamari to taste.

8. Serve immediately.

Kamasutra Curry

*Grilling the vegetables in this curry seems to help them
retain their bright colors.*

Yield: 6 servings
Time: About 30 minutes
12–15 minutes to grill

1 pound okra
1 teaspoon oil
1 1/2 cups chopped red onion (1 medium)
1 1/2 cups cubed red bell pepper (1 large)
1 teaspoon oil
2 cups chopped tomato (2 medium)
1 teaspoon oil
1 teaspoon tamari
1 teaspoon balsamic vinegar
1 tablespoon oil
1 tablespoon finely grated fresh ginger
4 cloves garlic, pressed
1 teaspoon cumin
1 teaspoon coriander
1 teaspoon pink peppercorns
1/2 teaspoon turmeric
1/4 teaspoon ground fennel seed
1/8 teaspoon cayenne
2 pounds cauliflower (1 large head)
1 1/2 cups water

1. Wash and chop the okra into 1/2-inch rounds, discarding the
   stem ends. Place the okra in a bowl with 1 teaspoon oil. Mix
   well to coat the okra with the oil. Place a rack with small holes
   over the bottom rack of your grill. Place the okra on the rack
   and cook over low heat for 6–8 minutes or until it is tender.

Turn the okra constantly as it cooks so it does not burn. Place it in a bowl and set it aside.

2. In another bowl, combine the onion and pepper. Add 1 teaspoon of oil and mix well. Place the vegetables on the rack and cook, turning often, for about 5 minutes or until the onion is tender. Add the cooked onion and peppers to the okra.

3. Place the tomato in the bowl in which you oiled the onion and pepper. Add 1 teaspoon oil, 1 teaspoon tamari, and 1 teaspoon vinegar. Mix well, and transfer this mixture to the grill. Immediately close the lid of the grill. Let the tomatoes cook for 1–2 minutes, and then turn them over with a spatula and let them cook for another minute. Place the grilled tomatoes in the bowl with the other vegetables.

4. In a large kettle, heat 1 tablespoon oil. Add the ginger, garlic, cumin, coriander, peppercorns, turmeric, fennel, and cayenne. Mix well and cook over medium heat for about 2 minutes. Add the cauliflower and stir until it is coated with the curry mixture. Add the water. Stir and bring the mixture to a boil. Cover and simmer until the cauliflower is almost tender. Add the grilled vegetables and simmer for about 5 minutes more. (The liquid in this recipe should be almost evaporated when it is done, but if the vegetables become too dry or start to stick, add a little more liquid.)

Serving Suggestion

Serve Kamasutra Curry with brown basmati rice and Chutney of the Seven Veils (page 88). It is also good with Bacall Burgers (page 135).

Dances with Chili Dogs

**Add vegetarian chili to tofu wieners
for a delicious Wild West favorite.**

Yield: 4 servings
Time: About 20 minutes to prepare
6–8 minutes to grill

*1 package of Yves Chili Dogs
(6 dogs, 275 g), thawed*

water sufficient to half cover the dogs

1/2 large red onion, thinly sliced

1 green pepper, cubed

1 teaspoon oil

*3 Italian plum tomatoes, sliced and halved, or
1 medium tomato, chopped*

2 teaspoons oil

1 teaspoon tamari

1 teaspoon balsamic vinegar

*15-ounce can pinto beans (If you use canned
beans with a high salt content, reduce the
amount of tamari in this recipe to taste.)*

1/2 cup tomato juice

2 cloves garlic, pressed

1 teaspoon chili powder

1 teaspoon cumin

1 teaspoon basil

1 tablespoon + 1 teaspoon tamari

1 teaspoon balsamic vinegar

1. Place the hot dogs in a pan. Add enough water to half cover

them, and bring the water to a boil. Reduce the heat and simmer the dogs for 3–5 minutes. Drain and set aside.

2. Place the onion and pepper in a bowl. Drizzle 1 teaspoon of oil over the vegetables and mix well. Place a rack with small holes over the bottom rack of your grill and transfer the vegetables to the rack. Cook over medium-low heat, stirring constantly, for 2–3 minutes. Close the top of the grill and let the vegetables cook for 1 minute, then stir for about 1 minute more until the onion and pepper are tender. Transfer the vegetables to a large pan. Set aside.

3. In a medium-sized bowl, combine the tomatoes, 2 teaspoons oil, 1 teaspoon tamari, and 1 teaspoon balsamic vinegar. Mix well.

4. Place the hot dogs together on one side of the grill. Pour the tomato mixture onto the grill, next to the dogs. (*Be careful*, this may cause some flames.) Quickly close the cover of the grill and let the food cook for 1 minute or less. Open the grill and turn the hot dogs and the tomatoes. Cook over medium-low heat for 2–3 minutes more, or until the hot dogs are grilled all over.

5. Transfer the tomatoes to the pan with the vegetables. Chop the hot dogs into bite-sized pieces, then add them to the pan.

6. Add the beans, tomato juice, spices, remaining tamari, and vinegar to the pan with the vegetables and hot dogs. Bring the mixture to a boil. Reduce the heat and simmer for 1–2 minutes.

Serving Suggestion

Serve with whole-grain bread or cornbread.

Sizzling Seitan

*Here's a vegetarian dish
to satisfy a meat-and-potatoes lover.*

Yield: 4–6 servings

Time: 20 minutes to prepare

15–20 minutes to grill

2 pounds new potatoes
2 tablespoons olive oil
6 cloves garlic, pressed
2 tablespoons tamari
16-ounce jar seitan, drained
and cut into bite-sized pieces
1 teaspoon thyme
1 teaspoon savory
1/2 teaspoon caraway seeds
1 bell pepper, diced

1. Scrub the potatoes and cut them into bite-sized pieces. Steam the pieces or cook in a pressure cooker until they are just barely tender (3–5 minutes). Drain the cooked potatoes.

2. In a large mixing bowl, combine the oil, garlic, tamari, seitan, thyme, savory, and caraway seeds. Mix well and add the potatoes. Mix gently to coat the potatoes.

3. Place a rack with small holes over the bottom rack of your grill. Place the potato/seitan mixture on the rack and cook over medium heat, turning often, until the potatoes and the seitan are browned (about 10 minutes).

4. When the potato/seitan mixture is done, remove it from the grill and keep it warm.

5. Place the pepper on the rack and cook over low heat, stirring often, until tender (5–8 minutes). Add the pepper to the potato/seitan mixture. Mix and serve.

Camille's Combo

*Grilling the tofu and onions
makes this simple recipe special.*

Yield: 4 servings

Time: About 20 minutes to prepare

15–20 minutes to grill

*2 cups chopped onions
1 teaspoon oil
1 pound firm tofu, cut into bite-sized cubes
1 tablespoon tamari
1 tablespoon oil
1/2 teaspoon liquid smoke
1 pound broccoli flowerettes,
in bite-sized pieces*

Sauce

*1 tablespoon oil
3 tablespoons whole-wheat pastry flour
2 cups soy milk
1/2 teaspoon sea salt
1 tablespoon Dijon-style mustard
1 teaspoon tarragon*

1. In a mixing bowl, combine the onions with 1 teaspoon of oil. Mix well. Place a rack with small holes over the bottom rack of your grill. Place the onions on the rack and cook, stirring often, until they are tender (5–8 minutes). Place the grilled onions in a large kettle.

2. Place the tofu cubes in a mixing bowl. In a small bowl, combine the tamari, 1 tablespoon of oil, and the liquid smoke. Mix well and pour over the tofu. Mix to coat the tofu.

3. Place the tofu cubes on the grill and cook over low heat, turning often, until they are brown on all sides (approximately 10 minutes). Add the tofu to the kettle with the onions.

4. Steam the broccoli until it is just tender (8–10 minutes).

5. While the broccoli is cooking, make the sauce: Heat 1 tablespoon of oil in a saucepan. Add the flour and mix well. While stirring constantly with a wire whisk, slowly add the soy milk. Keep stirring and cook over medium heat until the sauce is thick. Add the salt, mustard, and tarragon.

6. Pour the sauce over the grilled tofu and onions in the kettle. Add the broccoli, mix gently, and serve.

Serving Suggestion

Camille's Combo is delicious with Excalibur Potatoes (page 111).

Saint-Amour Bourguigon

For a lovers' feast, prepare this tofu in red wine sauce with Saint-Amour, a famous beaujolais.

Yield: 6 servings
Time: 1 hour or more to marinate tofu
About 10 minutes to prepare
20–23 minutes to grill

*2 pounds firm tofu cut into 1-inch squares,
1/2-inch thick*

1 1/2 cups dry red wine

1/4 cup tamari

6 cloves garlic

1/2 cup water

1 large red or green bell pepper, cut into cubes

2 cups chopped onions

1 teaspoon oil

1 1/2 pounds mushrooms

2 tablespoons oil, divided

3 tablespoons whole-wheat pastry flour

1 teaspoon thyme

1 teaspoon tarragon

1/2 cup water

1. Place the pieces of tofu in a large shallow dish.

2. Mix together the wine, tamari, garlic, and water. Pour this mixture over the tofu and leave it to marinate for at least an hour. (If desired, the tofu may marinate for several hours but should be refrigerated if it is marinated for more than 2 hours.)

3. In a mixing bowl, combine the pepper, onions, and 1 teaspoon of oil. Mix well. Place a rack with small holes over the bottom rack of your grill. Place the vegetables on the rack and cook

over low heat, stirring often, until the onions are tender (5–8 minutes). Return to the bowl and set aside.

4. Clean the mushrooms and cut them into halves or quarters to make bite-sized pieces. Place them on the grill and cook, stirring often, for about 5 minutes or until they are done. Add them to the bowl with the onions and pepper.

5. Drain the tofu, reserving the liquid for later use. Place the pieces in a bowl. Add 1 tablespoon of oil and mix well to coat the tofu. Place the pieces on the grill and cook over low heat, turning as needed to keep them from burning, until they are nicely browned (about 10 minutes). Add the tofu to the bowl with the vegetables.

6. In a large heavy kettle, heat the remaining tablespoon of oil. Add the flour, thyme, and tarragon. Stir over medium-high heat to brown the flour. Reduce the heat to medium and add a little of the remaining marinade. Continue stirring until a paste is formed, and then gradually stir in the rest of the liquid. Bring the sauce to a boil.

7. Add the grilled vegetables and the tofu to the sauce. Add the remaining 1/2 cup of water. Mix and let simmer for about 5 minutes to blend the flavors.

Serving Suggestion

For a hearty meal that would please a meat-eater, serve Saint-Amour Bourguignon with Excalibur Potatoes (page 111) or Joie de Vivre Baked Potatoes (page 113). Accompany with a green salad.

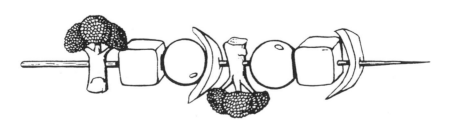

Helen of Troy Eggplant

Paris' love for Helen started the Trojan Wars.
This eggplant stew is good enough to fight over.

Yield: 4–6 servings
Time: 1 hour for eggplant to drain
About 35 minutes to prepare
10 minutes to grill

2 medium-sized eggplants
sea salt
1 tablespoon olive oil
1 cup chopped onion
12 cloves garlic, minced
1 1/2 teaspoons herbes de Provence
2 tablespoons tamari
20 sun-dried tomato halves
1 cup water
1 tablespoons olive oil
1 tablespoon arrowroot
1/2 cup water

1. Cut the eggplant into 1/2-inch-thick rounds. Lightly sprinkle each slice with sea salt. Stack the slices in a shallow dish and let them drain for about 1 hour.

2. While the eggplant is draining, prepare the other ingredients. Heat 1 tablespoon oil in a large kettle. Add the onion and the garlic. Sauté over low heat for about 20 minutes. Add the herbs, tamari, dry tomatoes, and 1 cup of water. Let simmer over low heat for about 10 minutes, stirring occasionally. Cover and set aside.

3. Rinse and dry the eggplant slices. Brush the slices on both

sides with the remaining oil. Place the slices on the bottom rack of the grill and cook over low heat until they are browned on the bottom (about 5 minutes). Turn them over and cook until tender.

4. Transfer the grilled eggplant to a cutting board and cut it into small cubes. Add cubed eggplant to the tomato sauce.

5. In a small bowl, combine the arrowroot and the remaining 1/2 cup of water. Mix well to dissolve the arrowroot. Pour this mixture into the stew. Bring it to a boil. Reduce the heat and let the stew simmer for 2–3 minutes.

Serving Suggestion

Serve this dish over a bed of brown rice or with pasta. Accompany with a big green salad.

Lancelot Tempeh

Enjoy a dish that's hearty, nutritious, and easy to make.

Yield: 4–5 servings
Time: About 20 minutes to prepare
10 minutes to grill

2 packages tempeh (8 ounces each),
thawed if frozen and cut into 1-inch cubes
2 cups halved, medium-sized mushrooms
1 red pepper, cut into 1-inch pieces
1 green pepper, cut into 1-inch pieces
1 cup halved and thinly sliced onion
2 tablespoons olive oil
2 tablespoons tamari, or to taste
4 cloves garlic, pressed
1 teaspoon sage

Sauce

1 tablespoon Dijon-style mustard
2 tablespoons honey
1 cup water
1 tablespoon arrowroot
1 tablespoon tamari
pinch of cayenne, to taste

1. Steam the tempeh for about 10 minutes

2. In a large bowl, combine the steamed tempeh, mushrooms, red and green peppers, and onion.

3. In a small bowl, combine the oil, 2 tablespoons tamari, garlic, and sage. Mix well and pour this mixture over the tempeh/vegetable mixture. Mix well. Place a rack with small

holes over the bottom rack of your grill. Transfer the tempeh mixture to the rack and cook over low heat, turning often, until the tempeh is grilled and the vegetables are tender (about 10 minutes).

4. Return the cooked tempeh and vegetables to the bowl and keep them warm while you make the sauce.

5. In a saucepan, combine all the sauce ingredients and mix well. While stirring constantly, bring the sauce to a boil. Cook and stir for a minute or so until the sauce thickens. Pour the sauce over the grilled tempeh and vegetables. Mix gently.

Serving Suggestion

Serve over a bed of brown rice or whole-grain pasta.

Anna Karenina Stroganoff

Now you can enjoy a rich and creamy Stroganoff without the cream.

Yield: 6 servings
Time: About 40 minutes to prepare
18–25 minutes to grill

2 pounds new potatoes
1 tablespoon oil
2 cups coarsely chopped onions
1 teaspoon oil
1 1/2 cups medium-sized mushrooms, cut into halves
16-ounce jar seitan, drained
and cut into bite-sized chunks
2 teaspoons oil
12 ounces fresh green beans, cleaned

Sauce

1 package (10.5 ounces) extra firm silken tofu
2 tablespoons white or yellow miso
1/2 cup soy milk

1. Scrub the potatoes and cut them into halves or quarters, depending on their size. Steam or pressure cook until the pieces are just barely tender but still firm (3–5 minutes).

2. Drain the potatoes and place them in a mixing bowl with 1 tablespoon of oil. Gently stir to coat the potatoes with oil. Place a rack with small holes over the bottom rack of your grill. Place the potatoes on the grill and cook over medium heat, turning often, until they are nicely browned (about 5 minutes). Transfer the potatoes to a large kettle and set aside.

3. In a medium-sized bowl, mix the onions with 1 teaspoon of

oil. Grill the onions over low heat , stirring often, until they are tender (5–8 minutes). Add the grilled onions to the grilled potatoes.

4. Place the mushrooms and seitan in a mixing bowl and add the remaining 2 teaspoons of oil. Mix well. Grill the seitan and mushrooms together, turning occasionally, until the seitan is crispy and the mushrooms are done (5–8 minutes more). Add the seitan and mushrooms to the kettle with the potatoes and onion. Set aside.

5. Steam the green beans until just tender.

6. While the green beans are cooking, make the sauce: Place the tofu, miso, and soy milk in a blender or food processor. Blend until smooth and creamy. If necessary, scrape the sides of the blender or food processor with a rubber spatula to make sure that the tofu is well blended. Add this mixture to the grilled vegetables in the kettle.

7. Place the kettle either on the grill or over medium heat on your stove to warm the stew. Stir until the stew is hot, but do not boil.

8. Serve garnished with the green beans.

❧ *BARBECUE TIDBIT* ❧

If you are serving an entire meal of grilled foods, serve it in courses. It is impossible to have everything ready at the same time, and most of the dishes in this book (except for soups, stews, pâtés, and salads) are best hot off the grill. ❑

Empress Eggplant

*The purple eggplant reminded me of a story
about a courtesan of ancient times who so beguiled
the emperor that he married her. When the couple's
subjects stormed the palace, the empress supposedly
refused to flee, saying, "These purple robes
are shroud enough for me."*

Yield: 4–6 servings
Time: 30–40 minutes to prepare
About 15 minutes to grill

*2 medium-small eggplants
(about 3/4 pound each)
1 1/4 cups chopped onion
4 teaspoons oil, divided
1 1/2 cups cooked brown rice
2 cloves garlic, pressed
1/2 cup tomato sauce
3/4 cup pitted black olives, chopped
2 tablespoons tamari
1 teaspoon oregano
1/8 teaspoon ground cloves
pinch of cayenne*

1. Wash the eggplants and cut them in half lengthwise. Using a paring knife, cut the flesh away from the center of each egg-plant half, leaving a shell that is at least 1/2-inch thick. Chop the flesh and set the shells aside.

2. In a mixing bowl, combine the onion and 2 teaspoons of olive oil. Mix well to coat the onion with the oil.

3. Place a rack with small holes over the bottom rack of your grill. Place the onion on the rack and cook over low heat, stirring often, for 3–5 minutes.

4. Place the chopped eggplant flesh in the bowl in which the

onion was mixed and add the remaining 2 teaspoons of oil. Stir to coat the eggplant with the oil. Add the eggplant to the onion and cook, stirring often, until both the onion and eggplant are tender (about 5 minutes).

5. In a large mixing bowl, combine the grilled onion/eggplant mixture with the cooked rice, garlic, tomato sauce, olives, tamari, oregano, cloves, and cayenne. Mix well.

6. Use this mixture to stuff the eggplant shells. Place the stuffed eggplants in a lightly oiled metal baking dish (such as a large cake pan), and cover it with aluminum foil.

7. Place the baking dish on the top rack of your grill over low heat. Cover and cook for about 15 minutes. The eggplant shell should be tender but still hold its shape. If it is not tender, cook for a few minutes more.

Serving Suggestion

Serve with some grilled tofu or tempeh and a big green salad.

Eggplant Rouletini

*These little eggplant rolls require more work
than most of our recipes, but they are still
easy to make and really good.*

Yield: 4 servings
Time: 1 hour for eggplant to drain
30 minutes to prepare
5–10 minutes to grill

*1 medium-large eggplant
sea salt
3 tablespoons tomato paste
3 cloves garlic, pressed
1/2 teaspoon dry mint
1/2 teaspoon oregano
1 cup grated soy cheese
2 tablespoons olive oil*

1. Cut the eggplant in lengthwise slices that are 1/4–1/2-inch thick. Make the first and last slices thinner and discard them. Lightly sprinkle the slices with sea salt and stack them in a shallow dish. Let the eggplant drain for 1 hour. Rinse and dry the eggplant slices.

2. Steam the eggplant slices about 2–3 at a time until they are just tender enough to roll. Make sure not to over-cook them or they will fall apart. (The steamer rack of a wok works well in this step.)

3. In a small bowl, combine the tomato paste, garlic, mint, and oregano.

4. Spread each eggplant slice with the tomato mixture and sprinkle it with the grated cheese.

5. Roll up the slices, like a jelly roll, starting at the smallest end.

6. Place the rouletini, seam sides down, on a plate and brush them
    with olive oil. Place the rouletini on the bottom rack of the grill
    and cook over low heat until they are brown on the bottom (3–5
    minutes). Turn them over and cook on the other side.

Serving Suggestion

Eggplant Rouletini can be made in advance and grilled just before
serving. This dish is delicious with Madonna Sauce (page 81).

Bolero Peppers

*Red and yellow peppers with a stuffing of black beans
create a dramatic and colorful effect.*

Yield: 4–8 servings

Time: About 20 minutes to prepare

15–20 minutes to grill

4 large bell peppers (2 yellow and 2 red)
1 tablespoon olive oil
1 cup chopped onion
1 teaspoon chili powder
1 teaspoon cumin
1 teaspoon basil
1/2 teaspoon oregano
2 cups cooked and drained black beans
1 tablespoon wine vinegar
2 1/2 cups cooked long-grain brown rice
1 teaspoon sea salt
1 cup chopped fresh tomato
8 slices cheddar-style soy cheese (optional)
water sufficient to cover bottom of baking dish

1. Cut the peppers in half lengthwise. Remove the stems and seeds.

2. Heat the oil in a skillet. Add the onion and sauté for about 3 minutes. Add the chili powder, cumin, basil, and oregano. Continue to sauté until the onions are tender (3–4 minutes more). Add the beans, vinegar, rice, salt, and tomato. Mix well.

3. Stuff the peppers with this mixture, packing them well. Top each pepper with a slice of soy cheese, if desired.

4. Place the stuffed peppers in a metal baking dish with about 1/4 inch of water in the bottom of the dish. Cover the dish with aluminum foil and place it on the top rack of your grill. Cook over medium-low heat for 15–20 minutes, or until the peppers are tender but still hold their shape.

Serving Suggestion

Enjoy Bolero Peppers plain or topped with some hot or mild salsa. Complete your meal with homemade cornbread and a green salad with slices of avocado.

Pomme d'Amour

At one time, the French called a tomato "pomme d'amour."
You're sure to love this simple but pretty tomato dish.

Yield: 4 servings
Time: 20 minutes to prepare
15 minutes to grill

4 medium tomatoes, ripe but still firm
1 1/2 cups cooked long-grain brown rice
1 tablespoon vegetable bouillon powder
1/4 teaspoon sea salt, or to taste
1 teaspoon basil
1/2 teaspoon oregano
2 tablespoons finely chopped parsley
1–2 cloves garlic, pressed
2 tablespoons grated parmesan cheese
or tofu parmesan

1. With a sharp paring knife, cut a circular opening in the top of the tomato. Using a small spoon, carefully scrape the pulp and seeds out of the center of the tomato, leaving a shell of flesh under the skin. Reserve the pulp for later use.

2. In a mixing bowl, combine the rice, vegetable bouillon powder, salt, basil, oregano, parsley, and garlic. Mix well. Add 1/2 cup of the reserved tomato pulp and mix again. (The remaining pulp can be used in soups or sauces.)

3. Carefully stuff the tomato shells with the rice mixture. Sprinkle with the parmesan. Place the stuffed tomatoes in an oiled metal baking dish and cover with aluminum foil. Place the dish on the top rack of your grill and cook over medium-low heat for about 15 minutes, or until the tomatoes are just tender but still hold their shape. Serve immediately.

Serving Suggestion

This tomato dish is a great accompaniment for grilled tofu or tempeh.

Fellini's Fettuccine

*This grilled mushroom and onion dish
tastes much more fattening than it really is.*

Yield: 4–5 servings
Time: 35 minutes to prepare
10 minutes to grill

*2 packages (10.5 ounces each) firm silken tofu
2 tablespoons tamari
water sufficient to cook pasta
1 recipe Don Quixote Mushrooms and Onions
(page 116)
8 ounces whole-grain fettucine
2 tablespoons minced parsley*

1. Place the tofu and the tamari in a food processor. Blend until smooth and creamy. Set aside.

2. Put a large kettle of water on to cook the pasta. Cook according to the directions on the box while the vegetables in step 3 are cooking.

3. Follow the recipe for Don Quixote Mushrooms and Onions.

4. Place the tofu mixture in a large saucepan and add the hot grilled mushrooms and onions. Stir the sauce over medium heat until it is warm, but don't bring it to a boil.

5. When the pasta is done, place it on individual serving plates and top it with the mushroom sauce. Sprinkle with some minced parsley. Serve immediately.

Midsummer Night's Squash

Enjoy a bright rendition of stuffed summer squash.

Yield: 4 servings	
Time: About 30 minutes to prepare	
15 minutes to grill	

Vegetables

4 medium yellow squash
1 stalk celery, finely chopped
1/2 cup chopped onion
1 teaspoon olive oil
1 small red pepper or 1/2 large, diced
1 cup corn, cut off the cob

Sauce

1/2 cup raw unsalted cashews
1 cup water
1/2 cup grated soy cheese
1/4 teaspoon nutmeg
pinch of cayenne
1 teaspoon sea salt

1. Wash the squash and cut each one in half lengthwise. Using a teaspoon, scoop the flesh out of the center of each squash half, leaving a 1/2-inch-thick shell. Reserve the scooped-out flesh for use in soups, stews, or other dishes.

2. In a medium-sized bowl, combine the celery, onion, and olive oil. Stir to coat the vegetables. Place a rack with small holes over the bottom rack of your grill. Place the celery/onion mixture on the rack and cook over low heat, stirring often, until the onion becomes translucent (5 minutes). Add the red

pepper and cook until the vegetables are tender (5 minutes). Place the cooked vegetables in a mixing bowl, add the corn, and set aside.

3. Now make the sauce: In a blender, combine the cashews, water, soy cheese, nutmeg, cayenne, and salt. Blend until very smooth and creamy. (If you don't blend the mixture long enough, the cashews will be gritty.)

4. Transfer the blended mixture to a saucepan and cook over medium heat, stirring constantly, until the sauce is very thick.

5. Add the sauce to the bowl with the grilled vegetables and mix well.

6. Fill the squash shells with this mixture and place them in a lightly oiled, metal baking dish. Cover the dish with aluminum foil. Place the baking dish on the top rack of your grill, cover, and cook over low heat for about 10 minutes. Check for doneness. The squash shells should be tender but not mushy. If they are not tender, cook them for a few minutes more.

Wuthering Heights Pie

Leeks, the national vegetable of Wales,
join with onions in this pie.

Yield: One 9-inch pie (6 servings)
Time: 1 hour to prepare
10–15 minutes to grill
45 minutes to bake

Crust

1 cup whole-wheat pastry flour
1/4 cup oil
3 tablespoons hot water

Filling

3 medium leeks
1 tablespoon olive oil
2 1/2 cups chopped onion (1 large Spanish)
1 tablespoon olive oil
3 tablespoons whole-wheat pastry flour
1 cup soy milk
1 tablespoon Dijon-style mustard
1 teaspoon thyme
1 teaspoon basil
1/2 teaspoon sea salt, or to taste
pinch of cayenne
1/8 teaspoon nutmeg
1/2 cup pitted black olives, cut into halves
1/2 cup pitted green olives, cut into halves
1/2 cup grated soy cheese

1. Prepare the crust: Place the flour in a medium bowl. Measure the oil and hot water into a small bowl. Do not mix. Slowly poor the oil and water over the flour, mixing with a fork just enough to form a ball.

2. Place the dough between two sheets of waxed paper and roll it out. Lightly sprinkle your work surface with water to keep the paper from slipping. (Don't sprinkle with too much water, or the paper will stick to the dough.)

3. Carefully peel off the top sheet of waxed paper. Pick the dough up by the corners of the bottom paper and place it (paper side up) in the pie pan. Carefully peel off the paper.

4. To clean the leeks, make an incision through the leek from top to bottom. Hold the leek open under running water to rinse out any sand or dirt. Chop the leek, using only the white and the light green part (You should end up with 4 1/2 cups of chopped leek.) Place the leek in a large mixing bowl.

5. Add 1 tablespoon olive oil and the chopped onion to the bowl with the leeks. Mix well to coat the vegetables with the oil. Place a rack with small holes over the bottom rack of your grill. Place the onion/leek mixture on the grill and cook over low heat until tender (about 10–15 minutes). Transfer to a mixing bowl.

6. In a saucepan, combine the remaining tablespoon of oil with the flour. Mix well. While stirring constantly with a wire whisk, gradually pour in the soy milk to make a sauce. Cook over medium heat, stirring constantly, until the sauce is very thick. Add the mustard, thyme, basil, salt, cayenne, and nutmeg. Mix well.

7. Add the sauce to the grilled leeks and onion. Mix well. Transfer the mixture to the crust. Flute the edges of the crust, smooth out the mixture in the crust, and decorate it with the olives. Top with soy cheese.

8. Bake at 350°F for about 45 minutes or until the crust is golden brown and the filling is firm. Let sit for about 10 minutes before slicing.

Marlene Dietrich Kebobs

The sauerkraut gives these kebobs a German accent.
Try them on a cool autumn evening.

Yield: 8 kebobs (4–8 servings)	
Time: 1 hour to soak skewers	
About 25 minutes to prepare	
10 minutes to grill	

8 bamboo skewers
24 small new potatoes
1 large Spanish onion, cut into 1-inch chunks
8 tofu hot dogs
4 cups sauerkraut
1 teaspoon caraway seeds
2 tablespoons oil
2 tablespoons tamari
1 teaspoon herbes de Provence

1. Soak 8 bamboo skewers in water for 1 hour before using.

2. Scrub the potatoes and steam or pressure cook until they are just starting to get tender. (Don't over-cook them or they will fall off the skewers.) Steam the onion pieces until they just start to get tender (4–5 minutes).

3. Cut each hot dog into 3 pieces. Thread the ingredients onto the skewers. Make sure that each skewer gets 3 pieces of hot dog, 3 potatoes, and 2–3 onion pieces.

4. In a metal baking dish, mix together the sauerkraut and the caraway seeds. Cover the dish with aluminum foil.

5. In a small bowl, combine the oil, tamari, and herbes de Provence. Brush the oil mixture over the kebobs. Place the kebobs on the bottom rack of the grill and place the dish of

sauerkraut on the top rack. Cook over low heat for about 10 minutes or until the vegetables are tender and grilled. Turn the kebobs occasionally so that they brown evenly. If there is any leftover oil/tamari mixture, baste the kebobs with it as they cook. When the kebobs are done, the sauerkraut should also be done.

6. Place the sauerkraut on a platter and top it with the kebobs.

Serving Suggestion

Serve with Dijon-style mustard.

Tropical Kebobs

*These colorful kebobs will delight your palate
as well as your eyes.*

Yield: 4 kebobs (4 servings)

Time: 1 hour to soak bamboo skewers

and marinate tempeh

About 35 minutes to prepare

8–10 minutes to cook

4 bamboo skewers
8-ounce package tempeh, thawed if frozen
1 large red onion, cut into 1-inch chunks
*1 recipe Sarong Sauce (page 73),
do not thicken*
1/2 large red pepper, cut into 1-inch squares
1/2 large green pepper, cut into 1-inch squares
*1/2 fresh pineapple, cored
and cut into 1-inch chunks*
2 tablespoons oil

1. Place 4 bamboo skewers in water to soak for 1 hour.

2. Cut the tempeh into 12 equal squares. Place the squares in a vegetable steamer. Place the onion chunks over the tempeh. Steam the tempeh and onion for 8–10 minutes.

3. Set the onion aside and place the tempeh in a shallow container. Follow the recipe for the Sarong Sauce skipping step 2. Pour the unthickened pineapple mixture over the tempeh. Let marinate for 45–60 minutes.

4. Thread the tempeh, onion, peppers, and pineapple onto the skewers in an alternating fashion. Make sure that each skewer gets 3 pieces of tempeh.

5. Brush the kebobs lightly with oil. Place a rack with small holes over the bottom rack of your grill. Place the kebobs on the rack and cook over low heat for about 8–10 minutes or until nicely grilled. As the kebobs cook, brush them with the marinade once or twice. Turn the kebobs occasionally so they will cook evenly.

6. Thicken the leftover pineapple mixture with the arrowroot (see step 2 on page 73).

Serving Suggestion

Serve the kebobs on a bed of long-grain brown rice. Top with Sarong Sauce.

🐦 *BARBECUE TIDBIT* 🐦

To make food preparation quicker, cook with a friend. One person can prepare foods, make sauces, and put things together, and the other can watch the grill. ❑

Oriental Kebobs

*High in protein, these tofu, tempeh, and seitan kebobs
are a great accompaniment to a lighter dish.*

Yield: 8 kebobs (6–8 servings)
Time: 1 hour to marinate tofu and soak skewers
About 45 minutes to prepare (while tofu is marinating)
10 minutes to grill

8 bamboo skewers

Sauce

1/2 cup water

3 cloves garlic

1 teaspoon rosemary

1/4 cup tamari

1 teaspoon freshly grated ginger

1 1/2 tablespoons arrowroot

Kebobs

1 pound tofu, cut in 1-inch cubes

*1/2 pound tempeh, thawed if frozen
and cut in 1-inch x 1/2-inch cubes*

water sufficient to cover bottom of pot

1 large red onion, cut in 1-inch cubes

1/2 pound seitan, cut into bite-sized cubes

16 medium mushrooms, cut into halves

2 tablespoons oil, or less as needed

1. Soak 8 bamboo skewers in water for at least 1 hour before
   using.

2. Mix together all the ingredients for the sauce except for the
   arrowroot.

3. Place the tofu in a shallow dish and pour the sauce over it. Let marinate for at least 1 hour while you prepare the other ingredients.

4. Place the tempeh in a vegetable steamer. Place the vegetable steamer in a pot with about 1/2-inch of water in the bottom. Cover and bring to a boil. Reduce the heat and steam the tempeh for about 10 minutes.

5. Remove the tofu from the sauce with a slotted spoon and briefly dip the tempeh in the sauce. Set aside tofu and tempeh.

6. Steam the onion cubes for 3–4 minutes.

7. Make the kebobs by alternately placing tofu cubes, tempeh, onions, seitan, and mushrooms on the skewers until the ingredients are used up. Set the kebobs aside while you finish preparing the sauce.

8. Add the arrowroot to the liquid in which you marinated the tofu and tempeh. Mix well to dissolve the arrowroot. Place the sauce in a saucepan. While stirring constantly, bring the sauce to a boil. Remove from the heat and set aside.

9. Brush the kebobs with the remaining oil. Place a rack with small holes over the bottom rack of your grill. Place the kebobs on the grill and cook over low heat, turning often, for about 10 minutes or until the vegetables are tender and the tofu, tempeh, and seitan are browned.

Serving Suggestion

Serve these kebobs over a bed of brown rice and top with the sauce. Accompany with a green salad.

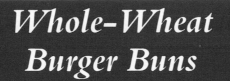

Whole-Wheat Burger Buns

Although these buns are not grilled,
they're perfect partners for the burgers in this chapter.

Yield: 12 buns
Time: 40 minutes to prepare
2 hours to rise
20 minutes to bake

1 1/4 cups lukewarm water
2 tablespoons concentrated fruit sweetener
2 tablespoons oil
1 tablespoon dry active yeast
1 teaspoon sea salt
1/2 cup gluten flour or 2 tablespoons
Vital Wheat Gluten
2 3/4 cups whole-wheat bread flour
(approximately)

1. In a large bowl, combine the water, sweetener, oil, and yeast. Let sit for 10 minutes to dissolve the yeast.

2. In a smaller bowl, mix together the salt, gluten flour or Vital Wheat Gluten, and 1 cup of the bread flour. Add this mixture to the liquid mixture and beat 100 strokes. Add as much of the remaining flour as necessary to make a kneadable dough. Turn the dough out onto a floured surface and knead for at least 10 minutes. Keep the surface sprinkled with flour to prevent the dough from sticking. Continue kneading until the dough is smooth, elastic, and only slightly sticky.

3. Oil the bowl in which you mixed the dough and return the dough to the bowl. Turn it over to oil the top. Cover the bowl

with a clean, damp cloth and let the dough rise in a warm place until it has doubled in bulk (about 1 hour).

4. Punch the dough down. Roll the entire piece of dough into a long cylinder (as if you were making a "rope") and cut it into 12 equal pieces. Shape each piece into a ball and place the pieces on a cookie sheet. Leave enough room between the pieces for them to double in size. Slightly flatten each piece of dough with the palm of your hand. (You can also shape the dough into hot dog buns. The baking time will be the same.) Let the dough rise until it has doubled in bulk (about 1 hour).

5. Bake at 350°F for 20 minutes. Cut the buns in half to serve with your favorite burger.

Desserts

Looking for a low-fat dessert that's as simple as it is sweet? Grilled fruit is for you! The natural sugar in the fruit caramelizes as it cooks, which makes the fruit seem sweeter. Garnish grilled fruit with a sprig of fresh mint or some nice red berries. Add a sweet sauce and maybe a scoop of homemade sorbet and you have a gourmet delight. Try different fruits with different sauces; for example, Carmen Carob Sauce (page 209) is for fruit kebobs, but it is also good over grilled bananas, other grilled fruits, or Cleopatra's Cake (page 196). Selene's Sorbet (page 206) is delicious with Simply Sublime Cobbler (page 200) and so on. A sprinkling of Sucanat is also nice over grilled fruit.

When making grilled fruit desserts, it is important to start with the best quality seasonal fruit. It should be ripe but not overripe. Tasteless, out-of-season fruit will not be good grilled or any other way. Fruits with a high water content—berries, grapes, and melons—are not good for grilling, but apples, peaches, pears, pineapple, plantain, bananas, and even fresh figs may be grilled. To grill fruit, just brush it lightly with oil and place it on the bottom rack of the grill. For small pieces of fruit, use a rack with small holes. Cook the fruit over medium heat for 3–4 minutes, turn it over, and cook for a couple of minutes more.

Several recipes at the end of this section are prepared without using your grill. Although not barbecued, each of these desserts is the perfect ending to a cookout. And they're all just too good to ignore!

Scented Garden Fruit Kebobs

Make this light and easy dessert a little richer
by serving with a sauce.

Yield: 6 servings
Time: 1 hour to soak skewers
About 15 minutes to prepare
5 minutes to grill

6 bamboo skewers
1/2 fresh ripe pineapple, peeled and cored
2 bananas
2 apples
1 tablespoon mild-flavored oil
(sunflower, safflower, or canola)
6 teaspoons Sucanat

1. Soak 6 bamboo skewers in water for 1 hour before you begin.

2. Cut all the fruit in 1-inch chunks. Alternate chunks of different fruits on the skewers. Place the kebobs on the bottom rack of your grill and cook over medium heat for about 5 minutes or until the fruits are hot and lightly browned. Be careful not to over-cook.

3. Sprinkle each kebob with 1 teaspoon of Sucanat. Serve immediately, plain or with Carmen Carob Sauce (page 209).

Serving Suggestion

If fresh figs are available, they make a delicious addition to these kebobs.

Fruit de Soma

According to the mythology of India,
soma is an intoxicating beverage that gives Indra,
the fertility god, his strength. When using the fruits
Indra bestows, make sure to choose fruit that is fresh,
sweet, and ripe, but not too ripe. The success of this
recipe depends on the quality of the fruit.

Yield: 6 servings
Time: 1–2 minutes to cook
3–4 minutes to grill

Sauce

1 cup unsweetened pineapple juice

1 teaspoon arrowroot

1/3 cup raisins

1 1/2 teaspoons freshly grated ginger

2 tablespoons fruit-sweetened
orange marmalade

Fruit

1 banana (not too ripe), cut in 1-inch-thick slices

1–2 apples, diced

1 pear, diced

1/2 ripe pineapple, peeled, cored, and diced

2 tablespoons mild-flavored oil
(sunflower, safflower, or canola)

1. In a saucepan, combine the pineapple juice, arrowroot, raisins, ginger, and marmalade. Mix well to dissolve the arrowroot and the marmalade. While stirring constantly, bring the mixture to a boil. Reduce the heat and simmer for 1–2 minutes or until the sauce is thick. Cover the saucepan and reduce the heat to minimum, just to keep the sauce warm while you grill the fruits.

2. Place the fruits in a large bowl and add the oil. Mix well. Place a rack with small holes over the bottom rack of your grill and transfer the fruit to the rack. Cook over medium heat, turning often with a spatula, until the fruit is hot and lightly browned (3–4 minutes).

3. Return the fruit to the bowl, add the sauce, and mix gently. Serve immediately.

Serving Suggestion

This salad is delicious all by itself but is *divine* with a scoop of nondairy, vanilla-flavored frozen dessert (such as Rice Dream).

Rhett's Dream

Rhett Butler had his Georgia peach, now you have yours—and each is a dream-come-true.

Yield: 4 servings
Time: About 10 minutes to prepare
1–2 minutes to cook
3–4 minutes to grill

1/2 cup raw, unsalted cashews

1 cup water

1/3 cup honey

1 tablespoon arrowroot

1 teaspoon vanilla

2 large ripe freestone peaches, peeled, halved, and pitted

1 teaspoon mild-flavored oil (sunflower, safflower, or canola)

1. Place the cashews and water in a blender. Blend at high speed for about 1 minute. Pour the resulting liquid through a fine wire strainer into a saucepan. Discard any large cashew pieces that are left in the strainer.

2. Add the honey, arrowroot, and vanilla. Mix well to dissolve the arrowroot and honey. While stirring constantly, bring the mixture to a boil. Reduce the heat and simmer until the mixture forms a thick pudding (about 1–2 minutes). Cover the pudding to keep it warm while you grill the peaches.

3. Brush the flat, cut side of the peaches with the oil and place them on the bottom rack of the grill. Cook over medium heat until they are browned on the bottom and hot all the way through (about 3–4 minutes).

4. To serve, divide the pudding among four plates. Place a peach half, grilled side up, in the center, on top of the pudding, and garnish with a sprig of mint or a ripe strawberry.

Serving Suggestion

The pudding may be made in advance and reheated; however, it has a tendency to form lumps when it is cool. If you wish to prepare the pudding in advance, it would probably be easier to make the cashew cream and cook it just before grilling the peaches. If you do need to reheat the pudding, add a tablespoon or two of soy milk, place over low heat, and stir vigorously with a wire whisk until the pudding is hot and smooth.

❧ *BARBECUE TIDBIT* ❧

When grilling vegetables or small pieces of fruit, it is very nice to have a wire basket or rack with small holes and sides. Sometimes called a "wok topper," it is great for making grilled "stir-fries." The vegetables will not fall over the sides as they do on the rack with the small holes. You can use this instead of the rack with small holes when grilling chopped vegetables. ❑

Nirvana

A coconut pudding as rich-tasting as one
made with milk and eggs is simply heavenly
over grilled pineapple and bananas.

Yield: 6 servings

Time: About 25 minutes to prepare

6 minutes to grill

1/2 cup finely shredded unsweetened coconut
1 cup water
3 tablespoons arrowroot
1/3 cup honey
1/2 package (10.5-ounces) extra firm
silken tofu
1 teaspoon vanilla
3 small bananas
1 pineapple, peeled and cored
1 teaspoon mild-flavored oil
(sunflower, safflower or canola)

1. Place the coconut and the water in a blender. Blend on high speed for about 1 minute. Place a fine wire strainer in a saucepan and pour the blended mixture through the strainer. Using your hands, press the coconut against the strainer to squeeze out the remaining liquid.

2. Add the arrowroot and the honey to the coconut milk. Mix well. While stirring constantly, bring the mixture to a boil. Let it boil for a few seconds and then remove from the heat.

3. Place the tofu in a blender. Add the vanilla and the cooked coconut milk mixture. Blend until smooth and creamy, using a rubber spatula to scrape the sides of the blender. Chill if the dessert is to be served later, or keep the mixture warm if it is going to be served as soon as the fruit is grilled.

4. Peel the bananas and cut them in half lengthwise then in half crosswise to make 12 pieces. Slice the pineapple into 1-inch-thick half-rings. Lightly brush the fruit with the oil. Place the fruit on the bottom rack of the grill over medium heat. Cook for about 3 minutes or until it is lightly grilled on the bottom. Turn the fruit over and cook about 3 minutes more.

Serving Suggestion

To serve, arrange fruit on individual plates and top with sauce. If desired, sprinkle with 2 tablespoons lightly toasted coconut.

Pears Elegante

*Some believe a pure complexion and shiny hair
are the result of eating pears regularly. Pears do give you
lots of mineral salts, vitamins, and carbohydrates,
but you won't care when you feast on this dessert.*

Yield: 4–8 servings
Time: 20 minutes to prepare
1–2 hours to chill
10 minutes to cook
3–5 minutes to grill

Sauce

*1 1/2 cups boiling water
2 tablespoons dry mint
2 teaspoons agar-agar flakes
1/4 cup mild clover honey*

Fruit

*4 ripe pears
1 tablespoon oil
1–2 tablespoons Sucanat
fresh mint for garnish*

1. Pour the boiling water over the dry mint. Cover and let steep for about 15–20 minutes.

2. Place a fine wire strainer in a saucepan and pour the liquid through the strainer. Add the agar flakes and bring to a boil. Reduce the heat, cover, and simmer, stirring occasionally, until the agar is dissolved (about 10 minutes).

3. Add the honey and transfer the mixture to a container to chill. Refrigerate until the mixture is cold (1–2 hours).

4. Wash the pears and cut them in half lengthwise. Using a paring knife, cut out the cores.

5. Brush the cut side of each pear with oil and place the slices, cut side down, on the grill. Cook over medium-high heat for 3–5 minutes or until the cut side is roasted and the pears are heated through.

6. Place the hot, grilled pears, cut side up, on a plate or tray and sprinkle them with Sucanat.

7. Stir the sauce and place a spoonful on each dessert plate. Place a pear, cut side up, on top of the sauce. Garnish with a sprig of fresh mint and serve immediately.

Serving Suggestion

Make the sauce earlier in the day and grill the pears just before serving.

Tropical Chocolate Dream

Here's an easy dessert that will win any chocolate lover.

Yield: 4–6 servings
Time: 10 minutes to prepare
About 5 minutes to cook
10 minutes to grill

Sauce

1 cup freshly squeezed orange juice
1 tablespoon arrowroot
1 cup malt-sweetened, non-dairy chocolate chips; or carob chips
1/4 cup Sucanat
1 tablespoon grated orange peel, organic or omit

Fruit

1–2 ripe plantains, peeled and sliced*
1/2 tablespoon oil
1 fresh pineapple, peeled and cut into chunks
1/2 tablespoon oil

1. In a saucepan, combine the orange juice and the arrowroot. Mix well. Add the chocolate chips, Sucanat, and orange peel.

2. While stirring constantly, bring the mixture to a simmer. Cook until the sauce is thick and the chocolate chips have melted. Keep the sauce warm while you grill the fruit.

---

* Be sure the plaintains are ripe; if they are not, they will be starchy instead of sweet.

3. In a mixing bowl, combine the sliced plantain with 1/2 table-spoon oil. Mix well to coat the plantain with the oil. Place a rack with small holes over the bottom rack of your grill. Place the plantain slices on the grill and cook over low heat until they are brown on the bottom (about 3 minutes). Using a spatula, turn the slices over and cook them on the other side. Transfer the plantain to a bowl and set aside while you cook the pineapple.

4. Mix the pineapple with the remaining 1/2 tablespoon of oil. Place the pineapple pieces on the grill and cook over medium heat until they are hot (about 5 minutes).

5. Reheat the sauce, if necessary, and mix together the pineapple and plantain. Place the grilled fruit on individual serving plates and top generously with sauce. Garnish with a twist of orange, if desired.

Apples in Strawberry Sauce Forever

Sweet, hot apples with a cool, light sauce
make a delicious contrast you'll enjoy forever.

Yield: 6 servings
Time: 5 minutes to prepare
10 minutes to cook
5–10 minutes to grill
2 hours for sauce to cool

Sauce

1 1/2 cups apple-strawberry juice
1/4 cup maple syrup
2 teaspoons agar-agar flakes

Fruit

6 apples, sliced
1/2 tablespoon lemon juice
1 tablespoon cinnamon
1 tablespoon oil
1/4 cup Sucanat

1. Place the apple-strawberry juice, maple syrup, and agar in a saucepan. Bring the mixture to a boil. Cover, reduce the heat, and simmer, stirring occasionally, until the agar is dissolved (about 10 minutes). Transfer the sauce to a bowl and refrigerate until chilled.

2. Place the sliced apples in a bowl with the lemon juice, cinnamon, and oil. Mix well. Place a rack with small holes on the bottom rack of your grill. Place the apples on the rack over low heat and cook, turning often, until tender (about 5–10 minutes). Return the hot apples to the bowl and add the Sucanat. Mix well.

3. To serve, stir the sauce and place a generous helping on each dessert plate. Top with the hot apples and serve immediately.

Serving Suggestion

A sprig of fresh mint and a fresh strawberry on each plate make a pretty garnish.

Dulcinea's Apples

*Apples prepared this way are a healthy treat
that is perfect for the grill.*

Yield: 4 servings
Time: 10 minutes to prepare
10–20 minutes to grill

4 large cooking apples
1/2 cup walnuts
3/4 cup currants or raisins
1 teaspoon cinnamon
1/4 teaspoon nutmeg
1/4 teaspoon allspice
*2 tablespoons fruit-sweetened
orange marmalade*

1. Wash the apples. With a sharp paring knife, cut a well in the top of each apple. Use a small spoon to empty out the well until it is about 1-inch in diameter.

2. Place the nuts, currants, and spices in a food processor and blend. Add the marmalade and mix well. Fill the apple cavities with this stuffing, letting it mound over the top.

3. Place the stuffed apples in an oiled metal baking dish. Cover the dish with aluminum foil. Place the dish of apples on the top rack of your grill. Cook over medium-low heat for 10–20 minutes, or until the apples are tender.

Serving Suggestion

Enjoy these apples hot or cold.

Cleopatra's Cake

*Grilled fruit really dresses up
our light and tender eggless cake.*

Yield: 6–9 servings
Time: 20 minutes to prepare
25 minutes to bake
6 minutes to grill

*1 cup whole-wheat pastry flour
1/2 cup barley flour
2 teaspoons baking powder
1/2 teaspoon baking soda
1/2 cup Sucanat
1 tablespoon vegetarian egg replacer
1/3 cup water
1/8 teaspoon cream of tarter
1 teaspoon vanilla
1 teaspoon apple cider vinegar
1/3 cup oil
1/2 cup soy milk
Nirvana (recipe on page 189)*

1. Sift together, through a fine wire strainer into a bowl, the flours, baking powder, baking soda, and Sucanat. Set aside.

2. In a large bowl, combine the egg replacer and the water. Beat for about 1 minute with a wire whisk or fork. Add the cream of tarter, vanilla, and vinegar and continue to beat. Add the oil and soy milk and beat again.

3. Stir the flour mixture into the liquid mixture and beat with a wooden spoon, until the batter is well blended.

4. Pour the batter into a well oiled and floured 8-inch x 8-inch cake pan. Bake at 350°F for 25 minutes, or until a toothpick

inserted into the center of the cake comes out clean. Let the cake cool in the pan.

5. Top each piece of cake with Nirvana pudding and surround it with banana and pineapple slices.

Variations

Cleopatra's Cake on the Sauce

Follow the recipe for Cleopatra's Cake up through step 4. Pour hot Carmen Carob Sauce (page 209) over the cake. Serve it with grilled bananas. Instead of carob sauce, try the chocolate orange sauce from Tropical Chocolate Dream (page 192).

Rhett's Dream Cake

Prepare Cleopatra's Cake up through step 4. Follow the recipe for Rhett's Dream (page 187). Instead of grilling peach halves, slice the peaches before grilling them. Top the cake with a generous spoonful of pudding and surround it with peach slices.

End-of-Summer Delight

Prepare Cleopatra's Cake up through step 4. Place small squares of the cake on individual serving plates, top the cake with Debonair Delight (page 210). Grill apple slices (page 194), place them on one side of the cake, and place a ball of End-of-Summer Sorbet (page 208) on the other side. Garnish with a sprig of mint, if desired.

Cleopatra's Cake Forever

Prepare Cleopatra's Cake up through step 4. Prepare Apples in Strawberry Sauce Forever (page 193). Place small squares of cake on individual serving plates. Top with the strawberry sauce, surround with the grilled apples, and garnish with fresh strawberries.

Cake à la Eve

This cake actually bakes on a gas grill! (A charcoal grill may not get hot enough.) It's light, quick, and so delicious.

Yield: 6 servings

Time: 15 minutes to prepare

---

12 minutes to grill

---

2 tablespoons oil
2 apples, peeled and sliced
1 cup whole-wheat pastry flour
1 1/2 teaspoons baking powder
1/2 teaspoon baking soda
1/2 cup Sucanat
1 tablespoon vegetarian egg replacer (powder)
1/4 cup water
1/2 teaspoon cream of tarter
1 teaspoon vinegar
1 teaspoon vanilla
1/4 cup oil
1/3 cup soy milk

1. Oil a metal 8-inch x 8-inch cake pan with 2 tablespoons oil. Cover the bottom of the pan with apple slices. Set aside.

2. Into a mixing bowl, sift together the flour, baking powder, baking soda, and Sucanat.

3. In another bowl, combine the egg replacer, water, cream of tarter, vinegar, and vanilla. Beat with a wire whisk for about 1 minute. Add the remaining oil and continue to beat. Add the soy milk and beat again.

4. Add the flour mixture to the liquid mixture. Beat for just a few seconds to combine the ingredients and then pour the batter over the apples in the pan. Immediately cover the pan with aluminum foil. (Do not stretch the foil tightly over the pan,

but let it bubble up so that the cake will not touch the foil as it rises.)

5. Place the cake on the top rack of the grill. The needle of the heat indicator should read just slightly over medium. Cook for 6 minutes and then turn off the gas and let the cake cook for 6 minutes more without opening the lid of the grill. The cake is done when a toothpick inserted into the center comes out clean.

Serving Suggestion

This cake is heavenly with Selene's Sorbet (page 206).

Roasted Chestnuts

What could be better on a cool autumn day than hot chestnuts, fresh off the grill?

Yield: 4 servings (6–8 chestnuts per person)

Time: About 5 minutes to prepare

About 10 minutes to grill

24–32 chestnuts

1. With a small sharp knife, cut an X through the shell of each chestnut. (This will keep the nuts from exploding as they cook.)

2. Place the chestnuts on the bottom rack of the grill and cook over medium-low heat, stirring often, for about 10 minutes. (When the chestnuts are done, they will give off a sweet, fragrant aroma.)

3. Remove the chestnuts from the grill and let them cool just enough to handle. Shell before eating.

Simply Sublime Cobbler

Here's a case of what Kipling called "delight in simple things."

Yield: 6–8 servings

Time: 20 minutes to prepare

15–20 minutes to grill

5 cups sliced pears (5 medium)
1/4 cup date sugar
2 tablespoons mirin
1/4 cup oil
1/2 cup amazake
1 cup barley flour
1 teaspoon baking powder
1/4 cup Sucanat

1. In a mixing bowl, combine the pears, date sugar, and mirin. Mix well and transfer the mixture to a lightly oiled, metal loaf pan. Set aside.

2. In a mixing bowl, combine the oil and amazake. Mix well and set aside.

3. Sift together the barley flour, baking powder, and Sucanat. Add this mixture to the amazake/oil mixture. Spread this batter over the pear mixture in the loaf pan. Cover with aluminum foil. (Do not stretch the foil tightly over the pan, but let it bubble up so that the cake will not touch the foil as it rises.)

4. Place the pan on the top rack of your grill over low heat. Cook for 10 minutes. Remove the aluminum foil and continue cooking for 5–10 minutes more.

Serving Suggestion

Serve warm or cold, plain or with a topping of lemon or vanilla-flavored frozen Rice Dream.

Casbah Cakes

Inspired by Mid-Eastern cuisine,
this is a very exotic-tasting dessert.

Yield: 6 servings (12–15 patties)
Time: About 15–20 minutes to prepare
About 15–20 minutes for couscous to set
1–2 hours to chill before cooking
2–3 minutes to grill

Cakes

2 cups peach juice
(You may substitute apple or orange juice.)
1 cup whole-wheat couscous
2/3 cup pistachios, hulled
1/4 cup Sucanat
1 tablespoon arrowroot
2 tablespoons honey
2 tablespoons oil

Sauce

1/4 cup honey
1/4 cup peach juice (or the juice used above)

Garnish

3 tablespoons chopped pistachios (not toasted)
2–3 peaches, peeled, sliced, and grilled,
if desired

1. In a medium-sized pan, combine the juice and the couscous. Cover and bring the juice to a boil. Remove the pan from the heat and let sit for about 15 minutes or until all the liquid has been absorbed.

2. Meanwhile, place the pistachios in an ovenproof pan and bake

at 350°F until they are lightly browned (about 10 minutes), stirring occasionally so they cook evenly. (A toaster oven's small size makes it just right for this job.) Let the nuts cool for about 10 minutes and then grind them into a powder.

3. Transfer the couscous to a mixing bowl. In another bowl, combine the ground pistachios, Sucanat, and arrowroot. Mix well and add this mixture to the couscous. Add 2 tablespoons of honey and mix well. If the mixture is too hot to handle, cover and let sit until it is cool.

4. When the mixture is cool enough to handle, shape it into patties that are about 2 inches in diameter and 3/4-inch thick. Place the patties on a cookie sheet and put in the refrigerator to chill. The patties will be firm when they are cold (1–2 hours).

5. Before grilling the patties, make the sauce: In a small saucepan, combine the honey and juice. Mix and bring to a boil. Keep warm.

6. Brush the patties with oil, and place them on the bottom rack of the grill. Cook over low heat for 2–3 minutes, turn them over, and cook on the other side.

7. Place the grilled cakes on a plate (2 per serving), sprinkle them with chopped pistachios and peaches, and drizzle a tablespoon of sauce over the patties.

Libertine Lemon Pie

*Although not made on the grill, this cool, light dessert
is a perfect ending for a dinner of hot and spicy foods.*

Yield: One 9-inch pie (serves 8)

Time: 20 minutes to prepare

10 minutes to cook

1–2 hours to chill

1 cup Rice Dream Beverage
1 tablespoon agar-agar flakes
1 package (10.5-ounces) extra firm silken tofu
1/2 cup mild clover honey
1/4–1/3 cup lemon juice to taste
peel from 1/2 lemon, grated
2 teaspoons vanilla
1 Coconut Pie Crust (recipe on page 205), cooled

1. In a saucepan, combine the Rice Dream Beverage and the agar. Bring the mixture to a boil. Reduce the heat to simmer and cook, stirring often, until the agar flakes are completely dissolved (about 10 minutes).

2. While agar mixture is cooking, combine tofu, honey, lemon juice, lemon peel, and vanilla in a food processor. Blend until smooth and creamy. Use a rubber spatula to scrape sides of food processor from time to time to make sure that tofu gets well blended.

3. When the agar has dissolved, pour the hot mixture immediately into the food processor with the tofu mixture. Blend until well mixed.

4. Pour the mixture into the baked pie crust and refrigerate until the pie is firm (about 2–3 hours).

Serving Suggestion

Decorate the pie with sliced strawberries and kiwi.

Persephone's Pineapple Pie

What would summer be without Persephone—or sunny pineapple. Enjoy this baked pie at summertime barbecues.

Yield: One 9-inch pie (serves 8)
Time: 10 minutes to prepare
10 minutes to cook
20 minutes to bake
2–3 hours to chill

1 cup fruit juice (pineapple, apricot, mango, papaya, or apple)

1 tablespoon agar-agar flakes

1 package (10.5-ounces) extra firm silken tofu

1 teaspoon vanilla

1/3 cup honey

2 cups fresh pineapple, peeled, cored, and cut into small cubes

1 Coconut Pie Crust (recipe on page 205), cooled

1. In a saucepan, combine the fruit juice and agar. Bring the mixture to a boil. Reduce the heat to low and simmer, stirring often, until the agar flakes are completely dissolved (about 10 minutes).

2. While the agar mixture is cooking, place the tofu, vanilla, and honey in a food processor. Blend until smooth and creamy. Use a rubber spatula to scrape the sides of the food processor from time to time to make sure that the tofu gets well blended.

3. When the agar has dissolved, pour the hot mixture immediately into the food processor with the tofu mixture. Blend until well mixed.

4. Place pineapple in the baked pie crust. Pour the tofu cream over the pineapple. Refrigerate until the pie is firm (about 2–3 hours).

Coconut Pie Crust

Crisp and easy-to-make coconut crust is not grilled but is perfect with our pies.

Yield: One 9-inch crust

Time: 10 minutes to prepare

---

20 minutes to bake

1/2 cup barley flour
1/2 cup whole-wheat pastry flour
1/2 cup finely shredded unsweetened coconut
3 tablespoons + 1 teaspoon oil
2 tablespoons water

1. In a 9-inch pie pan, combine the barley flour, wheat flour, and coconut.

2. Gradually pour in the oil while stirring with a fork. Stir until the oil is well distributed throughout the mixture.

3. Add the water and mix.

4. Using your hands, press the dough over the sides and bottom of the pan.

5. Bake at 350°F for about 20 minutes. Cool before filling.

❧ *BARBECUE TIDBIT* ❧

When cooking with charcoal, start your fire with lumpwood and add several briquettes at a time. This way, your fire will be quick-lighting and long-cooking. ❑

Selene's Sorbet

When the moon comes up and the grilling is done,
enjoy a sorbet named for the moon goddess.
For the best results, use a juice extractor.
If you do not have one, you can use bottled apple juice.

Yield: 6 servings	
Time: 10 minutes to prepare	
10 minutes to cook	
3–4 hours to freeze	

3 tablespoons water
1/4 cup honey
2 cinnamon sticks
1 teaspoon whole cloves
4–5 medium-large apples or
2 cups unsweetened apple juice
1/2-inch-slice fresh ginger

1. In a small saucepan, combine the water, honey, cinnamon, and cloves. (If you do not have a juice extractor for step 2, add a slice of ginger to the honey mixture before you cook it.) Bring the mixture to a boil, reduce the heat and simmer, stirring occasionally over low heat for about 10 minutes.

2. While the mixture is simmering, juice the apples and the ginger. Reserve 2 cups of juice. (If you do not have a juice extractor, substitute 2 cups unsweetened apple juice for the apples.)

3. Strain the honey/spice mixture into a shallow container (we use an 8-inch x 8-inch cake pan). Add the apple/ginger juice. Mix and place in the freezer.

4. When the juice mixture is frozen solid (it should take 3–4 hours), break it into small pieces using a metal spatula, or cut it into chunks with a knife. Work very quickly so that the

sorbet does not thaw. Place it in a food processor and blend until the sorbet is whipped and there are no more chunks (1–2 minutes). Scrape the sides of the food processor from time to time to make sure that the mixture gets well blended.

5. Immediately transfer the sorbet back to the container in which it was frozen and place it back in the freezer until time to serve. This can even be done a day in advance, but the sorbet is better when served the day it is made.

Serving Suggestion

This sorbet is absolutely marvelous with Cake à la Eve (page 198), or with grilled vegetables.

End-of-Summer Sorbet

*You will need a juice extractor—not a grill—to make this
incredibly delicious sorbet.*

Yield: 6 servings
Time: 10 minutes to prepare
3–4 hours to freeze

*3 large apples
1/2 pint blackberries
1 large ripe pear
3 tablespoons red wine, optional
3 tablespoons honey*

1. Wash the apples, cut them into wedges, and remove the seeds.
    Run the wedges through the juice extractor. Wash the black-
    berries, turn off the juicer (this will keep the berries from
    flying all over when you try to juice them), place the berries
    in the hopper, and turn on the juicer. Push the berries through
    the hopper. Wash the pear, cut it into wedges, and run it
    through the juicer.

2. Place the juice in a shallow container (we use an 8-inch x
    8-inch cake pan). Add the wine, if desired, and the honey. Mix
    well.

3. Place the juice mixture in the freezer. When the mixture is
    frozen solid (3–4 hours), break it into small pieces, using a
    metal spatula, or cut it into chunks with a knife. Work very
    quickly so that the sorbet does not thaw. Place it in a food
    processor and blend until the sorbet is whipped and there are
    no more chunks (1–2 minutes). Scrape the sides of the food
    processor from time to time to make sure that the mixture gets
    well blended.

4. Immediately transfer the sorbet back to the container in which

it had been frozen and place it back in the freezer until time to serve. This can be done a day in advance, but the sorbet is better when served the day it is made.

Serving Suggestion

For an exquisite dessert, use this sorbet in End-of-Summer Delight (page 197). It is also wonderful plain or with Debonair Delight (page 210).

Carmen Carob Sauce

Enhance grilled desserts with a sauce made on the stove.
It's thick and creamy and not too sweet.

Yield: About 1 1/2 cups

Time: About 10 minutes to cook

1 cup unsweetened carob chips
1 cup soy milk
2 teaspoons vanilla extract
1/3 cup Sucanat

1. Place all the ingredients in a heavy saucepan. Cook over medium heat, while stirring constantly until the carob chips are melted and the sauce is creamy.

2. This sauce will thicken as it cools. Before serving, reheat, adding a little soy milk to thin to the desired consistency.

Serving Suggestion

Enjoy with Scented Garden Fruit Kebobs (page 185) or grilled bananas.

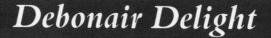

Debonair Delight

What's more debonair than blackberry brandy?
Our blackberry sauce.
Prepare it in your kitchen to enjoy over grilled desserts.

Yield: About 3/4 cup
Time: About 5 minutes to prepare
13 minutes to cook

1/2 pint blackberries, cleaned
1/2 cup fruit juice (apple, pear, or peach)
1 teaspoon arrowroot
2 tablespoons honey

1. In a saucepan, combine the blackberries and juice. Bring the mixture to a boil. Reduce the heat and simmer, stirring occasionally, for about 10 minutes.

2. Place a fine wire strainer in a bowl. Using the back of a wooden spoon, push the mixture through the strainer. Discard the seeds. Return the mixture to the saucepan.

3. In a cup or small bowl, combine the arrowroot and the honey. Mix well and add to the sauce. Bring the sauce to a boil. Reduce the heat and simmer the sauce for about 3 minutes.

Serving Suggestion

This sauce is not supposed to be very thick; it has more of a syrupy consistency. Serve it over Cleopatra's Cake (page 196), or over End-of-Summer Sorbet (page 208).

Index